How to Put the ❧ LOVE Back into ❧ Making Love

Books by Dagmar O'Connor

How to Put the *Love* Back into
Making Love

How to Make Love to the Same Person
   for the Rest of Your Life (and Still Love It)

How to Put the LOVE Back into Making Love

Dagmar O'Connor

Director, Sex Therapy Program
Department of Psychiatry
St. Luke's-Roosevelt Hospital Center

Doubleday

New York   London
Toronto   Sydney   Auckland

Published by Doubleday, a division of
Bantam Doubleday Dell Publishing Group, Inc.
666 Fifth Avenue, New York, New York 10103

DOUBLEDAY and the portrayal of an anchor
with a dolphin are trademarks of
Doubleday, a division of Bantam Doubleday Dell
Publishing Group, Inc.

LIBRARY OF CONGRESS CATALOGING-IN-PUBLICATION DATA

O'Connor, Dagmar.
  How to put the love back into making love / Dagmar O'Connor.
1st ed.
    p.   cm.
  1. Sex. 2. Sex in marriage. 3. Love. 4. Intimacy (Psychology)
I. Title.
HQ21.027 1989
613.9′6—dc19   88-18044
                                                          CIP

ISBN 0-385-24063-5

Book design by Kathryn Parise

Printed in the United States of America
February 1989
First Edition
BG

For H.P.

Acknowledgments

I want to thank my friend and collaborator, Daniel M. Klein, without whom this book could not have been written.

For professional advice and criticism, I want to thank Ruth Maxwell, Lothar Gidro Frank, M.D., and Alexander Elder, M.D.

I also want to express my appreciation to my friends Jeffrey Sandler, April Singer, and Birgitta and Stu Tray for their critical comments; to Sylvia Lachter, Sarah Busk and William Mears for support; to my agent, Mel Berger; to my legal adviser, Lawrence Gould; and to my editor, Jennifer Brehl.

Special thanks to Ian and Eric for putting up with Mom and another book.

D.A.O.

Contents ⚘

Contents

Introduction 🐍

"We've lost that loving feeling."

That refrain seems to echo in my office these days. Couples come to me saying that they can "do sex" all right—their "equipment" still works—it's "making love" that's the problem.

And it can be a heartbreaking problem.

Somewhere along the way *sex* and *love* have broken apart and all the books on improving sexual technique and attaining "super orgasm" can't put them back together again. We may end up more sexually adept, but we remain emotionally hungry.

Something is still missing. A connection to one another. A sharing of feelings. *Intimacy.*

My goal as a sex therapist has always been to find the way to genuine *lovemaking*—to discover how to get loving feelings flowing again and to integrate those feelings with a satisfying sex life. Just "fixing" a sexual problem can leave the heart unmoved. Sex, it turns out, is often just another way of avoiding intimate feelings.

My first book, *How to Make Love to the Same Person for the Rest of Your Life,* focused on a perennial problem, how to keep sex alive in a committed relationship. It examined the myriad ways that the routines of an everyday relationship can put the kibosh on a free, relaxed, and varied sex life. *How to Put the **Love** Back into **Making** Love* is the flip side of that book. It examines why we separate love from sex—how we suppress our emotions to "get through" sex and how we use purely genital sex to avoid loving feelings. But most important, this book offers my basic "recipe" for putting love and sex back together again.

🐛

How to Put the **Love** *Back into* **Making Love** is a response to the young woman who said to me: "These days sex just makes me feel lonelier and lonelier. Like it exaggerates how little there is going on between me and my husband."

And it's a reply to the middle-aged man who asked me: "How can I force myself to make love when I feel like I've got no 'love' left to make?"

And it's a guide to the hundreds of men and women who come to me wanting to know: "Can I ever feel real sexual intimacy again?"

My answer is a resounding *Yes!* If you are willing to try, the program offered in this book can lead you to a realm of sexual intimacy you have probably never experienced before.

But the truth is, I expect my program to give you much more than that. By learning (or relearning) how to make love with genuine feeling, I am confident that you can *improve every aspect of your relationship—in and out of the bedroom*. By tapping directly into your most intimate feelings, you can cut right through the layers of guilt and recrimination and dependence and resentment which may have been building between you and your partner for years.

Recently, my practice has included an increasing number of conventional psychotherapists and their spouses who are experiencing sexual problems. As I guided these couples through the Graduated Sensual Exercises, they were amazed to find a whole spectrum of changes in the way they related to one another: they began to listen to one another more patiently, to communicate more easily, to argue less and laugh more. But what really astounded these therapists was that they were also expanding as *individuals,* feeling more joy and spontaneity and romance in every aspect of their lives.

"I feel marvelous except for one thing," a psychoanalyst told me with a laugh as he came to the end of my program. "How can I go back to giving purely verbal therapy when I know that one touch is worth a thousand words?"

Indeed, many couples I know who have been joylessly "discussing their relationship" for as long as they can remember, finally break through to truly intimate contact with each other when they follow my prescription to "shut up and let your bodies make friends."

After reading my first book, people from around the world wrote to me saying how well I understood their problems. Yet a great many of them concluded by saying I told them everything *about* their problems, but not enough about what to *do* about them. *"How* do we change?" they asked. *"What* precisely can we do to improve our love life?"

🌿

As in my first book, *How to Put the* **Love** *Back into* **Making Love** will rely heavily on case material I have gathered in over seventeen years as a sex therapist at a hospital, a university, and in private practice with both couples and individuals. Part II in particular will draw on experiences in my Sexual Expansion Workshops with couples who "function normally" yet who feel they want more—especially more feeling—from their sexual relationships. Again, I will take the only approach I know: a belief that most of us share similar problems even if our "symptoms" differ; and a conviction that warmth, patience, and humor go a long way in helping us overcome these problems.

In the first half of this book, "Who Took the Love Out of Making Love?," I will examine the reasons why so many of us dissociate love from sex. I will take a hard look at "love anxiety," the various fears in which it is rooted, and the way it separates "doing sex" from "making love." I will show how our preoccupation with "having it all" has given us One-Minute Marriages in which we efficiently squeeze sex into our schedules and in the process squeeze feeling out of our relationships. I will document how gender myths, both old and new, continue to dissociate love and sex; the male, "Tough Guys Don't Smooch" myth, and the female, "Liberated Women Don't Have Heartthrobs" myth. I will show how bartering sex for love and love for sex can deprive a relationship of all feeling—both heartfelt and sensual. And in "Unfaithfully Yours," I will show how confusing sex for love can compound the dilemma of infidelity. I will demonstrate how, in an era of legitimate sexual fears, safe sex offers a "silver lining" of liberating sexual frankness and a renewed concern for the emotional component of sex. And finally, I'll look into what it means emotionally and practically to merge love and sex.

Part II will guide you, step by step, through the Graduated Sensual Exercises, a "hands-on" therapy that stirs the emotions, a route through the senses that goes directly to the heart. These are a set of exercises that release our capacity to feel and express love by exploring our sensuality. It is a program that works—in fact, it works wonders if you let it. In the first chapter, "Let's Skip This Part of the Book, Okay, Hon?," I will address you and your partner's natural resistance to trying these exercises and show how much you have to gain by overcoming that resistance. In "I Want to Be Touched Now," I will detail Week One of the exercises, and in "Different Strokes for Different Folks," I will run through the variety of joys and cop-outs you may have experienced that first week. Next, in "Making a Mess of Your Love Life," I will show you how to take the exercises to the next level of sensuality in Week Two, how you can release inhibitions by changing simple habits, and how you can get your whole body tingling by experimenting with new ways of touching one another. In "Sharing Your Most Intimate Secret," I will show you how to break through the ultimate emotional and sexual barrier to true intimacy. And in "Beautiful Fruit" and "Show and Tell, Touch and Go," I will lead you step by step into genital adventures that are at once erotic and unthreatening. Finally, in "The Love You Make," I will show how what you have experienced in these exercises becomes integrated into an ongoing lifelong love affair.

Recently, a young woman told me that she felt as if she were about to swoon as she glimpsed a couple in a passing cab urgently and lovingly kissing each other.

"After the Sexual Revolution is done and gone, that's still what it's all about," she said to me. "I still want those kinds of feelings, that kind of love."

I know exactly what she meant.

We've all seen countless books on the mechanics of genital sex which claim to be about making love. But my feeling—and the feelings of most of the people I know—is that those books have got it all backward. It's our hearts we're worried about, not just our genitals. And that is why I have written this book.

 PART I

Who Took the Love Out of Love Out of Making Love?

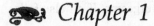 *Chapter 1*

Are You Doing Sex or Making Love?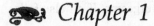

"Was it good for you?"

"It was okay."

"Just okay? But I was sure you had a . . . you know."

"Orgasm? I had two of them."

"Great! So what's wrong?"

"I just feel kind of empty. And lonelier than before we started."

"Oh. Maybe we should do it again."

Doing sex is a perfect way to suppress our heartfelt feelings and to fake intimacy at the same time. We can go at it with gusto, flesh to flesh, reach thundering orgasms, and then convince ourselves that we've made deep, intimate contact with one another. After all, we've just made "love," haven't we?

But most of us aren't fooled for long. Often, we feel something is missing, something basic, and we begin to feel isolated, emotionally undernourished, and lonely.

So we try again. We *do sex* with ever greater gusto and expertise. We study up on G-spots and "sexual focus" points. We collect *erotica* and master *technica* that will encourage us to do it

3

more frequently and have more ecstatic orgasms. If all else fails, we seek a new sexual partner.

And then we feel even lonelier.

Because ultimately, just *doing sex* can *never* be a satisfying substitute for *making love*. Focusing on genital sensation and climax—on getting each other off and getting it over with—robs us of the best chance we have to feel like complete human beings.

All day long in the grown-up world we hold back our emotions; we act civilized instead of screaming in anger, yawning in boredom, or giggling at the absurdity of it all. Naked and alone with our partners, we yearn to feel whole again, to let our feelings run free. We yearn especially for those tender feelings, loving feelings—feelings that allow us the magic of merging with one another if only for a few hours.

"Don't go mystical on us, Dagmar," I can hear someone in the back row protesting. *"All you are really saying is there's a big difference between doing it fast and doing it slowly, aren't you?"*

I hope I'm saying a great deal more than that, yet it will probably take this entire book for me to make the difference between *doing sex* and *making love* completely clear. But, yes, it *is* true that making love takes time. It begins with an attitude that allows us to take our focus off genitals and orgasms and to languorously contact one another with a whole spectrum of feelings—sensual and emotional as well as sexual.

These are the feelings that love is made of.

They are also the feelings that scare the hell out of us.

The Sensual Therapist

In all the years I have been practicing therapy, never have so many people come to me saying that "loving feelings" are missing from their sexual relationships. Men and women tell me that they feel "numb" with their partners, that they feel like distant observers in their own bedrooms, that the only way they feel "turned on" is by fantasizing about someone else. "Something's seriously wrong with me," they confess miserably. "I can't feel."

Yet at the same time never have more couples come to me who have constructed their lives and their relationships in such a way that it is virtually impossible for them to have regular and sustained sensual contact with one another. Without realizing it, they have figured out how to avoid the prime source of the very feelings they yearn for.

These couples want me to bring back their loving feelings by "fixing" a sexual problem they are having or by teaching them how to "do it" better.

"Forget sex," I tell them. "Right now, that's only getting in the way of your feelings. What you need—what we all really need— is to learn how to make sensual contact with each other. Once we bring that into our lives, sex and love will follow naturally."

A sex therapist who says "Forget sex"?

That's me. Maybe I should change my title to "Dagmar O'Connor, *Sensual* Therapist." For in my experience, sexual feelings, marvelous as they are, are only a fraction of the rich range of feelings that real *lovemaking* can produce.

Real lovemaking lets our feelings and body sensations run free, unfettered by "ideas" about sex. It is easy for us to see how sex and love were separate in Victorian times: the former was "dirty," the latter was divine, and ne'er the twain could meet. But this same split still exists—albeit in a different way—in our own times. Sex is no longer immoral—in fact, it's "good" to be erotic and sexually athletic and proficient—yet eroticism still has little to do with our feelings of intimacy.

When we allow ourselves to leisurely caress each other's bodies from head to toe, when we linger with arousal instead of hurrying on to "the next step," numbness gives way to sensation and the boundaries that separate us start to crumble. Layer upon layer of defenses drop, pockets of anger and mistrust float away. We face each other with a new and astounding nakedness. *This* is the feeling we were missing; *this* is the real intimacy that will end our feelings of loneliness. It stirs unconscious memories of the closest we have ever felt to another human being: we are like sensuous infants merging with our mothers.

And that is when our terror begins, the terror I call "love anxiety."

"Help! I Feel Too Good!"

Whenever a couple begins their first session by telling me about "this marvelous vacation" they had—long, amorous afternoons spent in the bed of their beachfront hotel room—I fear the worst. Invariably what follows is the story of a cruel fight on the flight home, weeks or months without any physical contact or with only perfunctory, impersonal sex, or worse, an infidelity the very week they returned home.

"How could he do it?" one woman cried to me. "Here we'd just had the tenderest, most loving week of our lives, made love for hours at a time, and two days later he's in bed with this woman he barely knows. He has no feelings at all!"

"On the contrary," I responded. "After all your intense love-making, he probably had more feelings than he could handle. 'Doing sex' with a stranger was his way of escaping those overwhelming feelings."

Similarly, coming home to a routine of no sex or unfeeling sex is a common way of putting the lid on overpowering feelings that were shaken loose by a period of unaccustomed lovemaking. It's unfortunate, but it's natural. Until you get used to these powerful new feelings—until you learn to be confident that they are in your control—you automatically back away from them. Love Anxiety is scary stuff.

The flip side of the wonderful closeness we feel when we make love is the terrifying vulnerability we feel. We do indeed feel like an infant in our mother's arms, but just beneath our sense of soothing comfort is our terror that she will swallow us up, strip us of our independent power and identity. We will lose control of all our emotions. Or, even more devastating, she will abandon us.

Most of us are familiar with that reflex that can snap us back to cold consciousness just as we are drifting off to sleep. It is most likely to happen when we are overtired and we start to drop into unconscious so fast that we feel like we are falling from a window. A similar reflex can bring us down with a smack just as we start to float off on a dreamy cloud of sensuality with our partner; we snap to, terrified of losing control. Somewhere in our preconscious we feel that if we don't get that control back quick, we will never get out of this bed; we will just caress and cuddle, suck and hold on to one another forever. We will be eternally trapped in this relationship. We feel that our need for this intimate connection is so big that if we go through with it, we will never be able to function as a mature adult again. *How can I, this oozing, voluptuous woman, ever go back to running the legal department or making dinner for five again?*

And so we nip those powerful feelings in the bud by going right back to doing sex. We focus on our genital sensations and aim directly for orgasm. Orgasm becomes a way of putting the lid on the whole experience, of bringing our emotions back under control.

"Oh God, what was I doing floating off in that sensuous dream? It's time to get back to business, back to the job at hand. Where was I? Ah yes—trying to make orgasms."

Contrary to the popular myth of sex and love, when you come, merging time is over. That's a physiological fact. When you are in the throes of orgasm, you *can't* focus on your partner, or anything else for that matter. You are all alone. As our foremost sexual sage, Woody Allen, puts it: "Love creates stress, sex relieves it."

The Loving Paradox:
Holding on While Letting Go

I believe that very few of us know how to make intimate love. It is a process involving many steps, most of which we habitually skip, physically *and* emotionally.

And that is an awful shame. Because today most of us feel the need for a loving connectedness more than ever. In a brutally competitive and risky grown-up world, we yearn for life's gentler qualities. We yearn for the solace and pleasures of intimate lovemaking.

Well, the happy news is, we can learn to have it all: intimate contact with one another *and* a strong sense of our own individuality. We can learn how to merge on a long, sensual afternoon *without* succumbing to our fear of being swallowed up. The trick is to learn how to completely let go of our emotions *while* remaining secure that we are completely in control of them. Only then can we return again and again to intimate pleasures without succumbing to the terrors of love anxiety.

We must start by recognizing our need to pull back into our shells when our feelings threaten to overwhelm us. It is a self-preserving reflex. Yes, after that marvelous vacation of day-upon-day of languorous lovemaking which left us raw with emotion, it makes perfect sense that we don't want to share a word, let alone a caress, on the trip home. Because, yes, for a little while, the boundaries between us did crumble, we did lose ourselves, and now we have to get ourselves back again—to come up for air. We need to cut ourselves off, to start planning a business trip, to turn our heads and read the paper, to talk with a stranger. And we have to recognize our partner's need to do the same without seeing it as rejection or betrayal or coldness.

Once we get that straight, once we can truthfully admit to each other that too much intimate contact can be scary, we won't have to come home to a self-made purgatory of months without physical contact or of perfunctory sex or, worse, of real sexual betrayal.

But how do we learn to make intimate love in the first place?

Through a series of Graduated Sensual Exercises that gently awaken our loving feelings while at the same time desensitizing us to the terrors of love anxiety. Step by step we allow these feelings to grow more powerful, to flow through us and between us. And every day as we get out of that sensual bed intact—in full control of our emotions—the more intimately we can merge the next time we get into it. Over the course of months, we learn the fine art of holding on while letting go. For those of us who are fortunate enough to be in an enduring relationship, it can be a life-changing experience which brings feeling and sensuality surging into every aspect of our life.

"Hold it right there, Dagmar," I hear dozens of you screaming. *"For years you've been haranguing us to stop taking sex so darned seriously and have some fun in the sack instead of always loading it down with 'meaning.' Now all of a sudden we're supposed to* make love *instead of just* doing sex. *What's going on? You're starting to sound like a pastoral counselor instead of a fun-loving sex therapist!"*

Don't misunderstand me. The last thing in the world I want is to turn your sex lives into a deadly serious business. Nor do I believe for one moment that we should give up those occasional lovely "quickies" or those erotic "rolls in the hay." But somewhere along the line too many of us have given up our most intimate emotions—sacrificed them to unfeeling sex—and that has left us numb and lonely.

And only making love can bring those feelings back again.

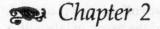 *Chapter 2*

The One-Minute Marriage

Craig C. entered my office ahead of his wife, Elizabeth, at a zippy, no-nonsense gait. A television producer who commutes to the West Coast weekly, Craig had emphasized on the phone that they would have to keep their appointment schedule with me flexible due to the demands of their respective jobs. Elizabeth is managing editor of a New York–based magazine.

"What brings you here?" I asked when we were all seated.

"I come too quickly," Craig blurted out, looking me straight in the eye.

I nodded back, not in the least surprised. After more than seventeen years as a practicing sex therapist, I have become rather adept at second-guessing this particular symptom in men. Craig fit the profile of a premature ejaculator perfectly: a quick walker and talker, an anxious man who got right down to essentials, he apparently behaved in bed the same way he behaved in the rest of the world. Except the bedroom was the one place where Craig was not rewarded for his efficient, first-to-finish behavior.

"You come too quickly for what?" I asked.

"For her, obviously," Craig responded, sounding a bit annoyed. "It's usually over for me in only a few minutes and she needs longer for her orgasm."

"At least five minutes longer," Elizabeth said, matter-of-factly. "Otherwise I'm left hanging with this unfinished feeling."

I looked at them. They were an unusually attractive pair in their mid-thirties, energetic, powerful, talented, the kind of high-achievement couple who are featured in the magazine Elizabeth edits. They were both geared to getting things done and this obviously included sex. Even Elizabeth spoke of their sex life in terms of a task to complete: she had clocked it down to five minutes before she could feel "finished." Both of them seemed to be saying to me: "Fix our sex life and fix it quick!"

I turned to Elizabeth. "I guess the most efficient solution would be for you to learn to come as quickly as Craig," I said with just the hint of a smile. "Maybe with practice we could get you both down under one minute."

They both stared at me incredulously and then, thankfully, they burst out laughing. It was laughter that signaled a first step toward a happier relationship, a glimmer of recognition that super-efficient sex has little at all to do with the pleasures of making love.

"Remember When Making Love Meant Spending the Whole Day in Bed?"

After the highly touted book *The One Minute Parent*, I expect it is only a matter of time before we see one titled *The One Minute Marriage*, a how-to handbook on fitting high-quality intimacy and sex into a tightly scheduled marriage. It would have one chapter on how to communicate efficiently with your partner—how to discuss the children, the bills, and your undying love for each other in concise, attention-getting sentences—and another on how to get your spouse to be a more productive worker in the marital "minicorporation." And, of course, the climactic chapter

11

would tell how to cut lovemaking down to essentials; how, indeed, to have *one minute sex.* Heaven knows, half the couples who come to see me these days seem to be looking for such advice—at least until I get a hold of them.

I can get severely cranky about "efficient" relationships. If there is one thing that makes me blow my therapeutic cool, it is an intelligent, well-educated couple who tell me that they each work seventy-plus hours a week (often not the *same* seventy hours), that they eat dinner separately more frequently than together, that after work they "de-stress" at separate health clubs, and then they want to know why their sex life isn't working. And, they ask me impatiently, how quickly can I fix it for them.

I want to scream at these One Minuters: "Making love isn't just another item on your checklist! It's not another job to do right! Doesn't anybody remember when making love meant spending the whole day in bed?"

It makes me feel terribly old-fashioned and, thank God, very romantic.

"I don't know what happened to us," a young data systems executive named Christine told me. "Bob [her husband] and I used to have sex two or three times a week no matter how busy we were. No problem. But about six months ago, it started tapering off and then it just stopped."

I soon discovered that this young couple were only awake together less than one hour each weekday night. Earlier in their marriage, they were able to "squeeze sex" into their allotted time together but then, as Bob put it, "I just lost the urge."

"I don't think the urge deserted you, you deserted it," I told him. "It doesn't sound like you were giving yourself enough time to feel much of anything, so your body just called it quits."

Later Christine admitted that she was so preoccupied with her schedule that her mind would start wandering to what was coming up *after* sex before they even got started.

"I'd think about all the things I had to do before tomorrow, and then I'd start worrying about whether I would get enough sleep," she said. "Soon my mind was skipping the sex part altogether. I could never just *be here now.*"

Despite all the propaganda that says that couples leading productive, independent lives have more relaxed relationships and put fewer demands on each other, the productive independent couples I know put the same old demands on one another—they just have a lot less time to satisfy them. With one eye on the clock, they have to cram in intimate talk and physical contact *besides* all the business of running their home and family. And the fact is, *our most intimate emotions and sensual feelings refuse to be rushed.*

When intimacy is put under a time restriction, something has to give and often it's our bodies that give up first. Increasingly, the sexual problems I see in my office are the casualties of an obsessive-compulsive lifestyle. These men and women are intent on being productive, on not wasting a minute, but their "inner child" is so starved for real loving that it rebels and as a result sex tapers off to nothing or he comes too soon or she doesn't come at all.

The way Craig and Elizabeth had scheduled their lives, Craig felt he could not afford the time to enjoy arousal, so he short-circuited it altogether by ejaculating within a few minutes after sex began. Premature ejaculation is almost always a symptom of anxiety-filled sex which has a mental stopwatch clocking it from the start. In a similar way, anorgasmic women are also often victims of their perceived pressures of time: they are so sure they will take "too long" to have an orgasm that they "give up" and have none at all. In earlier generations, both symptoms were bred in the back seats of parked cars and in basement rumpus rooms where the quicker sex was over, the less likely the young lovers were to be caught *flagrante delicto.* But these days, they seem to be bred in business schools and boardrooms; getting to the goal as fast as possible is the all-pervasive mind-set and it's hard to leave that mind-set outside the bedroom door.

Especially if your partner is in a hurry, too.

I suspected from the start that Elizabeth was as much a party to their slam-bang sex life as Craig was. When I began asking her some questions about her sexual habits—particularly about her preferred ways of achieving orgasm—she gave me short, somewhat petulant answers and finally said that none of this was "relevant" to the issue anyhow.

"I want to be supportive," she said, "but shouldn't you be working on Craig?"

"While you watch?" I responded. "That sounds a little bit like what's going on in your bedroom already."

At the end of that initial session, I asked them to try an experiment: "While Craig is in California this week, I want you each to promise to masturbate at least once."

As we will explore in greater detail in a later chapter, the very mention of masturbation can bring on paroxysms of self-consciousness and shame in most couples: it is our last "dirty little secret" from each other.

"You don't have to discuss it," I assured them. "Just do it and get it over with. You don't even have to spend much time on it."

I could tell from the moment they entered my office that next visit that there was less tension between them. Craig, in particular, appeared more relaxed.

"I feel like I had a little vacation from all that guilt about being a hair-trigger lover," he said, smiling. "Like I delegated some responsibility."

Indeed, he had delegated the responsibility for Elizabeth's orgasms to Elizabeth. And she, albeit more tentatively, admitted to feeling better, too. By not having to depend on Craig for her orgasms, she did not have to go around feeling "unfinished," frustrated, and angry. And by acknowledging that intercourse was not the only way Elizabeth could come, they *both* were now free to focus on arousal and all the feelings it elicits. The truth is, as a sex therapist I don't work on orgasms very much at all, don't worry about when or how people come or do not come; that all seems to take care of itself once we learn to fully enjoy the feelings that precede it.

"Now that you've got orgasms out of the way," I told them, "you can get on to the really important stuff—*making love.*"

But to make love, Craig and Elizabeth had to spend loads of time doing "nothing" with each other—not an easy task in a *One Minute Marriage.*

From Yuppie Love to Puppy Love

There is an old joke a friend in Sweden used to tell about a man named Sven who worked in a large Stockholm office. One spring, Sven's boss began leaving the office every Wednesday at noon. Within weeks, all Sven's coworkers were sneaking out right after the boss had left, but not Sven—he always remained dutifully at his desk until five sharp. Sven's colleagues teased him mercilessly about his slavish loyalty and finally one Wednesday Sven relented and left with the others. He drove home, let himself in, and climbed the stairs. He had just opened his bedroom door when he saw his boss in bed with his wife. Sven quietly closed the door, raced back to the office, and stayed until five. The following Wednesday, his colleagues asked him if he was going to take the afternoon off again.

"Not me," Sven said. "I almost got caught last time!"

Sven's topsy-turvy priorities don't seem any crazier to me than those of a great many couples I've come across recently. Again and again I am confronted by couples who make *Intimate Time Together the most expendable time on their schedule.* They find it much easier to say no to a date with each other in bed than to say no to a job opportunity or to a party invitation.

"I felt like we always could make up for lost time together

sometime in the future," one woman told me, "until one day I realized that year after year the only time we ever spent a whole morning in bed was during vacation. We'd practically postponed sex right out of our lives."

Marriage has always provided a perfect setup for avoiding sex and all the guilts and anxieties that accompany it. We could have a fight about the bills just before going to bed; we could blame the kids for never giving us any privacy; we could catch the eleven-o'clock news on the bedroom TV. But these days couples have found the ultimate no-fault solution to the intimacy problem: *they are hardly ever at home and awake at the same time.*

Craig and Elizabeth are typical of the couples I see who have programmed lovemaking right out of their lives. For others, the initial symptom may be different—she may have a diminished libido; he may be impotent; both may be "functioning fine" except for the fact that they have only had sexual relations once in the past eight months—but the common denominator is that *they are loath to permit themselves time for mere pleasure.* Coming quickly is simply one of the more "efficient" ways of doing sex—and avoiding most of the feelings of sensuous lovemaking. The whole game is over before it really begins: Oops, that's all, folks, and on we go to the next scheduled activity.

The next activity I scheduled for Craig and Elizabeth was the first of the Graduated Sensual Exercises. In Part II of this book, I will take you through these wondrous exercises in detail, step by step guiding you deeper into the realm of pure lovemaking. For now, I'll just say that the purpose of these exercises is to reacquaint us with the delicious pleasures of unhurried body contact: the joys of the lingering caress, of exploring an ear with a tongue, or feeling hair lightly brushing against a belly or thigh.

At the same time, these exercises are designed to gradually desensitize us to the anxieties that accompany prolonged intimacy—the fears of being "swallowed up" by our partner, of losing all control of our emotions, of never being able to function as an independent person again. Magically, as we rediscover the joys of unhurried sensuality, we start to "find time" for love-making in our lives. In fact, Intimate Time Together suddenly becomes the *least* expendable time on our schedule.

But the hard part is starting the exercises in the first place; for One Minuters in particular, the resistance is formidable.

Typically, One Minuters focus all their attention on what goes on in my office rather than on what goes on later in their bed-rooms. They arrive at my door exactly on time, listen to every word I say, and glance at the clock on the way out to make sure they've had the full hour they contracted for. Yet for weeks on end they never "find the time" to do the Sensual Exercises at home. One woman always arrived at my office clipboard in hand and took meticulous notes on everything said (she reminded me of those expectant fathers who watch the birth of their children through a camera lens so that they will not have to focus on it emotionally), but this same note-taking woman "forgot" for a month to do the first exercise I assigned her.

Frequently, a couple will protest that assigning these exercises as "homework" takes all the spontaneity out of sex. I remind them, as gently as possible, that the spontaneity went out of their overscheduled lives long ago.

"Let's get back in touch with pleasure," I say. "Then sponta-neity will come back spontaneously."

Often, both husband and wife will pester me to speed up the process. "We already *did* that exercise," they tell me. "Why can't we go on to the next one?"

As Thelonius Monk replied to the man who wanted to know what his jazz "meant," I say, " 'If you gotta ask questions, you aren't ready for the answers.' You'll only be ready when you're so relaxed that you're not hell-bent on going to the next stage."

Other couples are blunter: "I can't spare two or three hours a week for this stuff," they say. "Who's got the time?"

These are often people who get anxious if they are not doing at least two things at once: they cannot go jogging without listening to their Walkman—preferably to a course in macroeconomics. So I suggest that they turn the Sensual Exercises into a "research project."

"Draw a graph in your head about where you're most sensitive," I tell them. "Write yourself a memo on what you are feeling while she caresses you."

It starts as a familiar distraction, but soon he is focusing on himself in the here and now and the caress is more important than the memo.

To motivate some of these high-powered couples to start their homework, I have to talk turkey: "Don't you want to get your money's worth?" I ask them.

Who would have thought it would be so hard to sell people on sensuality?

The way a partner resists an exercise often flushes out a fundamental problem in the relationship. For Craig and Elizabeth's first week of exercises, I asked Elizabeth to be the first Initiator—the partner who decides when they will do it. The Initiator automatically becomes the *Touchee,* the person who lies back and receives the caresses for as long as he or she desires. I told Craig that he had to wait—no pestering allowed—for Elizabeth to take her turn before he could ask for his.

When they arrived for their next session, Elizabeth cheerfully informed me that she and Craig had had a wonderful week together, that she felt closer to him than in years. . . . But, incidentally, they had *not* done their homework.

"Were you afraid that trying the sensual exercise might disturb those close feelings?" I asked her.

Elizabeth raised her eyebrows as if I were talking nonsense. At the end of the hour, I asked them to try again the following week, Elizabeth still the Initiator.

Again, it didn't happen. Elizabeth said her work schedule had been "jammed" that week and that they had had houseguests at their country home on the weekend. I pressed her harder this time.

"Does the idea of just lying still and being caressed make you nervous?" I asked.

"No," she said, shrugging.

I looked at Craig. Instead of appearing unhappy—after all, Elizabeth's resistance to having sensual contact with him could easily be interpreted as rejection—he had a boyish smirk on his face. It was the look of vindication.

"She *never* can initiate anything just for pleasure," he blurted out loudly. "It's against her ethic. I have to beg her for hours just to go to the beach or to sit through a dopey movie. There's never time. There's always something more important to do."

At this point, Elizabeth broke down, tears flooding from her eyes. We had finally gotten down to basics.

All along, Elizabeth's actions and attitude had been saying to Craig: "You can't expect me to just lie in bed with you for an hour and not produce anything. I'm a serious person. I don't waste my time on anything as frivolous as sensual pleasure."

And so Craig, always the efficient worker who gave what was asked of him, had learned to come quickly, so Elizabeth would not have to "waste her time on pointless pleasure." Elizabeth had communicated her need to Craig subtly. She was not like the wife of one premature ejaculator I know who only wanted to make love just before they were due at a party—now *that* was a woman who knew how to set a stopwatch ticking loudly. It had taken Elizabeth's resistance to the Sensual Exercises to finally make Craig *conscious* of the stopwatch Elizabeth set on all pleasurable activity.

Yet Elizabeth did not really want Craig to ejaculate before she ever got started, the frustration born of that had sent her seeking help in the first place. She was stuck in the middle of her own contradiction: she wanted a *longer time* to reach orgasm, but *no time* for arousal. And it just doesn't work that way. If all we want is to "squeeze in" sex, we will inevitably "squeeze out" pleasure. For Elizabeth even to try the first exercise, she had to confront her deep fear of "surrendering" to sensuality: she was terrified; it meant she would lose her drive, her job, her control over life. In her mind, the only alternative to totally efficient Yuppie Love was mindlessly irresponsible Puppy Love.

But why was Craig smiling?

Yes, he had finally realized that he did not have to shoulder the entire blame for their unsatisfying sex life. But more significantly, the balance of power between him and his wife had shifted dramatically. Instead of being the one who took the kick out of sex, Craig had now positioned himself as the *Pleasure-pushing Person.* After all, Craig was the one who tried valiantly to get Elizabeth to the beach, and she, obviously, was the one resisting. She could not even initiate the Sensual Exercise, right?

As we will see frequently in succeeding chapters, couples have a knack for polarizing each other into the Pleasure-pushing Person vs. the Pleasure-resisting Person. "He's uptight," says the sexy-looking woman, dragging her husband into my office. "And I'm so loosey-goosey." But alas, these labels usually don't stick under close scrutiny. In fact, Craig was as resistant as Elizabeth to giving in to leisurely pleasure. But as long as Elizabeth actively resisted any pleasure Craig suggested, he could maintain his posture as the frustrated Pleasure Pusher without having to confront his own anxieties.

Still, Craig's smile and Elizabeth's tears offered them the opportunity to break through their resistance. I asked Craig to be the Initiator the following week and, of course, there was no way the Pleasure Pusher could refuse. For Elizabeth's part, she had finally recognized her resistance for what it was: fear. That was half the battle.

This time it worked: they were each able to "submit" to pleasure for fifteen minutes that week. And in the process they began to understand the two great lessons of the Graduated Sensual Exercises: Pleasure is its own reward; and it doesn't make you fall apart. Over the course of the following two months, Craig and Elizabeth found more and more time in their schedules to allow "pointless pleasure" to enter their lives, to "do nothing" together. As they gradually slowed down their lovemaking and started to appreciate the *process* of sensually contacting one another without focusing on the goal of orgasm, they began to think of Craig's original symptom—now cured—as a godsend.

"It sure got our attention," Craig happily told me. "My penis was the last romantic in my body. It was saying, 'Hey, either slow down or I quit.' It knew we were missing something wonderful."

Baby: The Ultimate Product

In Woody Allen's futuristic comedy *Sleeper*, Woody wakes up to a brave new world in which all reproduction is managed in the laboratory and all sex has been reduced to quick solo visits to an "orgasmatron": total efficiency. The audience roars.

The future is here. In response to the one out of six couples who suffer from infertility problems, reproductive technology has created a variety of amazing options: artificial insemination, *in vitro* fertilization, surrogate motherhood. For the infertile, these are miracles. But these laboratory wonders are no longer reserved just for the infertile; they have become options in the One Minute Marriage. For the super-efficient couple, laboratory-aided baby making guarantees product delivery on schedule without inconvenience—*including the "inconvenience" of making love.*

Reproductive issues have always come up in sex therapy. I frequently see women who are so terrified of pregnancy that

21

they can never completely let go in bed, often forfeiting orgasms in the process. Increasingly, I see men and women with infertility problems who have reduced their sex lives to the project of making a baby: the only sex they indulge in is intercourse, and they usually only do that when her temperature is just right. In both cases, I urge couples to first admit to themselves that they can enjoy sex that has nothing to do with reproduction. For a great many of us—religious or not—sex that is just for pleasure and is *explicitly* separate from reproduction can stir up powerful anxieties. That is why so many people resist trying sexual alternatives to intercourse: deep down inside they don't think they should be doing this stuff just for pleasure; that would be "unnatural." Similarly, there are many bright and sophisticated women who never completely educate themselves about contraception because that would force them to admit that most of the time they just want sexual pleasure, not a baby.

And so I have always urged couples to make a distinction between reproductive sex and recreational sex—between Making Babies and Making Whoopee. I tell them, "Once you accept the fact that you aren't really trying to make a baby every time you make love, you can start having sexual fun, in a variety of ways."

But then along came the One Minuters and I started having some second thoughts. For many of these getting-things-done couples, making babies and making love have become a little *too* separate. They see reproduction as another "efficiency" problem, Baby as another product to be produced.

"I'm thirty-six, my biological clock is ticking, and I'm up for an important promotion next year, so I want to have my baby before then," a publicist named Joanna told me. "That's why I'm going to the clinic for artificial insemination."

"But why are you *here?*" I asked.

Her husband lowered his eyes.

"Because we never make love anymore," he said.

I shook my head incredulously. It was as if their two problems —making love and making babies—needed two entirely different solutions. Did I have to lecture this high-powered pair on the birds and the bees?

"Here's my rule," I told them. "You can either wait until after you've had a baby by artificial insemination to start therapy, or you can wait for a year after you've finished therapy to start artificial insemination—that is, if you still need it. But you can't work on both problems as separate issues at the same time."

Joanna stared back at me angrily.

"I hope you'll choose to start working on your lovemaking first," I said. "Making love in hope of conceiving a child can be the most beautiful lovemaking there is. But neither love nor babies can be made in a hurry."

Slowing down was the best thing that ever happened to this couple. At last they were able to get into their feelings and a more active sex life followed naturally. Something else followed naturally. I am happy to report that a year and a half later, Joanna became pregnant—the old-fashioned way.

"It's a miracle," she told me happily on the phone.

Indeed it is—every time.

Fred, My Health Club

"I'm confused," a colleague said to me recently. "Half the people who come to see me are single and terrified that they're going to spend the rest of their lives alone. And the other half are marrieds who've rigged their lives so that they only see their spouses one night a week. Is that all the first half wants—a marriage that's like a three-hour date?"

In fact, I think both groups want a whole lot more than that. I have a pet theory that deep in their hearts these One Minuters are incurable romantics. In all these marriages where nobody is ever at home lurks a sensualist who really wants to stay at home all day—preferably in bed with his or her mate. We are running so fast because we yearn to lie still; we are living lives of super-independence because we yearn to be endlessly stroked and comforted like a child. And we are afraid that if we ever give in to all these yearnings, we will never be able to live independently again.

Yet many of the One Minuters I know are finally discovering that they never did gain true independence by spending less and less time together; they just gained a new form of loneliness and frustration—including sexual frustration. And as they now begin to spend more time together, much of it "doing nothing" in bed, they find they are developing a stronger yet calmer sense of independence when they get out of that bed.

"It's not like we've suddenly turned into country peasants or something," one reformed One Minuter told me laughingly. "But for starters, we both quit our health clubs so we could spend more time just hanging out together. Fred's my health club now. Yum."

 *Chapter 3*

Tough Guys Don't Smooch

The scenario repeats itself almost daily in my office.

SHE: [with fire and/or tears in her eyes] He never kisses me! He never fondles me! He won't even hold my hand! He always wants to get right down to business—the old in-and-out! He doesn't care about me. *The man just has no feelings at all!*

HE: [with befuddlement and/or resentment in his eyes] Of course I care about her! *But it's just impossible to make that woman happy.*

The variations are infinite, but the theme is always the same: he is cold and selfish and out of touch with his feelings and she is so starved for affection that she does not feel turned on by him anymore, cannot have orgasms with him anymore, or perhaps has simply given up making love to him altogether. And it is *all his fault.*

I should admit right off that I think men have been getting a bad rap lately. Every time I turn around, another psychological theorist is proving beyond doubt that 90 percent of men either hate women or, at the very least, are incapable of loving them. It is a self-serving theory: we women can then place the blame for unsatisfying relationships solidly on men; our only culpability is our supposed need to be victims. I think these theories are demeaning to both sexes. Most men, I've found, are as starved for love as women are; and most women I've seen are not so much masochistic as they are frightened of their own healthy aggression. True, the majority of men I see in my office do not express emotion or affection as easily as their partners do—*at least at the beginning of therapy*. And yes, most of these men are more focused on genitals and orgasms than their partners are—*at least at the beginning of therapy*. But behind every "cold and insensitive" man does not necessarily lie a love-starved "doormat" of a woman; very often that "doormat" is a woman who is keeping her own love anxiety at bay by encouraging her "cold-hearted lover" to remain that way.

"Heck, I'm No Sissy"

Arnold and Eva G. reminded me at once of the George Segal/ Sandy Dennis couple in the film version of *Who's Afraid of Virginia Woolf?* Arnold is a well-built man in his early thirties with a boyish handsomeness and brusque confidence which have served him well as sales executive for a textile company. Eva is his perfect opposite: diminutive, delicately pretty and shy, she spoke in a wispy, little-girl voice and seemed perpetually on the verge of tears. Indeed, her eyes were wet when she finally confessed to me that she had lost all interest in sex after a particular incident six months earlier.

"Arnold had been in Atlanta at a sales conference for a week," she began, "and the minute he came home, he started pawing me like a piece of meat. No kiss, no hug, nothing. He just dragged me off to the bedroom like a caveman and did it to me. It had nothing to do with me. I felt used and humiliated. It felt like rape."

"That was *passion*, not rape!" Arnold bellowed. "Do I have to be punished for the rest of my life because you turn me on?"

"Passion?" Eva cried. "You never even look at me; the only time we ever make eye contact is when you're lying on top of me. And you hardly ever talk. Heaven knows, it never feels like you really love me when we're having sex. And then you fall asleep with one leg over me like I'm a pillow."

"But I've told you I love you a hundred times," Arnold shouted. "We've been making love for ten years and you always had an orgasm. What's missing, for God's sake? *Women are never satisfied.* What do you want from me?"

"I want some romance," Eva whimpered.

At this point, Arnold threw up his hands. Here, to be sure, was a Tough Guy who could not even understand why anyone would *want* to smooch. He did not have the foggiest idea that anything was missing from their relationship; in fact, if Eva would only stop complaining and start having sex again he would be perfectly happy.

But in Eva's mind, that one night had become a symbol of everything that was missing in their relationship. For her, sex without affection was the equivalent of rape and so she had stopped wanting any sex at all. They were stuck, polarized: Arnold was a Sex Fiend and Eva was an Eternally Dissatisfied Woman. And for the six months following that traumatic night, they had each dug deeper into their ruts.

"It's like I'm afraid to turn my back on him," Eva said. "He's always pinching my bottom or grabbing my breasts or brushing up against me like a dog. I'm forever pushing him away."

"And you keep coming back for more?" I asked Arnold. "Sounds to me like you like being pushed away. Otherwise you'd approach her in a gentler way."

"Look," Arnold said, scowling, "I'm just not the romantic type and she knows it."

This thirty-four-year-old executive might just as well have said, "Heck, I'm no sissy."

"Be Sensitive, But Be a Real Man"

Tough guys are made, not born. It begins with Momma and is nurtured in the schoolyard. When a young boy takes his first steps toward independence from his mother, he is also taking his first steps in denying his need for maternal warmth and affection. At two or three, he already senses that he has to make a clean break from Mom or he will never grow up to be an independent and active man, like Dad; his sister, on the other hand, can continue to identify with "emotional" Mother as she reaches for independence. While still in overalls, the boy stakes out his identity as a Doer as opposed to a needy Feeler. The masculine split-off of Action from Feeling has begun, and as he grows, that breach will only get wider. In time, it will be the split off of Sex from Love.

Even in this feminist era, most little boys still grow up believing that hand-holding, hugging, and tender kisses are "sissy stuff" which only Momma's boys do. By the time he is pubescent, a boy's aversion to "feminine" feelings makes it virtually impossible for him to give or receive tender affection. He is terrified that affection will emasculate him—make him soft, feminine, even gay. Sex, of course, is something else. In his first schoolyard lessons about sex, he learns that masculine sex is active and aggressive; it is what a Man *does to* a Woman. A real man gets right *down*—literally horizontal—to business: sex begins with his erection and ends with his orgasm. Perhaps if he is truly considerate he will provide her with some foreplay; but that is strictly a manipulative means to the end, a priming of the pump, not something to be enjoyed in itself. Feelings have nothing to do with it.

But all along he has been suppressing his feelings, suppressing that need for nurturing, comforting, loving affection which he began denying so long ago. And the longer he suppresses that need, the larger it grows. It is like a dieter who has been denying his hunger for so long that the mere glimpse of a chocolate cake sends him into a panic. Often, a grown man's suppressed need for affection has grown so big that the minute he is lying in bed with his wife he becomes panicked that he will be overpowered by his need. His only alternative is to take action and take it fast: to *do sex!*

Traditionally, masculinity has been defined in opposition to femininity: men are hard, *not* soft; strong, *not* weak; active, *not* passive; rational, *not* emotional; in control, *not* vulnerable. And given this definition, a real man cannot allow himself to indulge in the feminine luxury of "pointless pleasure": of kissing and petting endlessly without aiming toward orgasm; of lying passively in bed for an hour while being lightly caressed; of being rocked like a child in his partner's arms; of sharing that intimacy that is far more profound than mutual orgasms—mutual tears. All of these pleasures are forbidden a real man—*they could turn him into a woman.* And that is his deepest fear. A man who indulges in these "feminine" pleasures is terrified that his "feminine" side will take over. He will go soft and weak: impotent. Or even worse, he will go gay. Both of these panics—fear of impotence and fear of one's own unconscious homosexuality—reside just below the surface in the most "normal" of men.

At some primal level, an erect penis remains the fundamental symbol and source of a man's power. It is his sword and scepter. The very word "potent" refers to all his strengths, political and financial as well as sexual. And a soft penis remains a symbol of exactly the opposite: weakness and incompetence. I am always struck by how totally humiliated a man can feel by his flaccid penis *even at those times when there is no reason in the world for his penis to be hard.* A case in point is the humiliation some men feel immediately after ejaculation when they naturally lose their erections. They experience what the French call *le petit mort*—"the little death"—as their tower of masculine strength tumbles down and slips out. Their potency is gone, spent. The sword is just a worm again.

Ironically, most men who experience impotency problems with their wives attempt to cure themselves by trying to do sex with ever greater determination instead of trying to come to terms with what they feel about their wives. "I'm just not doing it right," they think, instead of, "Maybe there is a reason why I don't *feel* like doing it with her at this time." Yet it is usually the split off of doing and feeling that got them into their predicament in the first place. Chances are their impotency is a symptom of some deep-seated anger that they have been unable to risk expressing out of fear of losing their partner. But that feeling has to come out before their penis will "do" anything.

Homosexual panic is just as insidious and even more limiting than impotency panic. Whenever *machismo* is on the rise in our culture—as it most certainly is again today—homosexual panic is always lurking near. The current preoccupation with the masculine "virtues"—with the hard and intrepid fighting man/patriot, with the heavily muscled body and the stubble-covered face, with the reprise of the strong, silent type as movie hero—is, I believe, related to the renewed stigma AIDS has placed on homosexuality. Today, heterosexual men who once felt secure and comfortable with their soft sides are again distancing themselves from all "feminine" behavior. It is no longer safe to be playful, sensitive, vulnerable, and sensual. A man has to be a Tough Guy just to survive.

Finally, there is no denying that the rise of women's power—in the office, in the home, even in the gymnasium—has had the unfortunate effect of pushing many men even further into denying their "feminine," emotional sides. How can they risk being emotional—and vulnerable—when it is hard enough as it is to "stay on top"? As women embrace the masculine "virtues," many men feel forced into becoming supermasculine men, and once again feelings are sacrificed in the process.

Arnold G. could not begin to acknowledge the existence of a gentle and sensitive side to himself or his own need for tender affection. When I saw him alone, I questioned him about his early upbringing and he described his father, a foundry worker, as "perpetually busy" and his housewife mother as "perpetually lonely." He recalled that his father used to leave for work the minute dinner was over, but his mother would keep Arnold at the table and "go on chattering about anything and everything. She used to say that I was a great listener which was pretty ridiculous considering that I tuned her out most of the time."

Starved for emotional contact, Arnold's mother had laid an incredible emotional burden on her young son, asking him to be the sensitive friend her husband never had been. Arnold remembered that his mother had made him promise her not to become a factory worker who would never be home with his family, a promise that only exacerbated Arnold's feelings of disloyalty toward his father.

"But it's not like she wasn't fond of the old man," Arnold was quick to assure me. "She was always bragging about how he was still stronger than all the younger guys at the foundry."

Very quickly I was getting the picture of a mother who had given her son that classic double message: *Be sensitive, but be a real man!*

"Your mother sounds like she was a hard woman to please," I said to Arnold.

"Impossible!" he said, throwing up his hands in the same gesture

31

of resignation with which he had responded to his wife's "impossible" demands.

He then leaned forward and, as if he were bringing up an entirely new topic, asked me, "What can I do to get Eva to respond to me? I'm desperate. I'll try anything you suggest."

I smiled at Arnold. Without realizing it, he had intuitively made the association between his mother and his wife. The man who could never please his mother now wanted to know the trick to pleasing his wife. He was asking the question men ask me most frequently: "How can I make my wife more responsive? What secret 'technique' will turn her on?" It is an endearing question, hardly Tough Guy talk at all, but my answer is almost always the same.

"For starters, *stop!*" I said to Arnold. "Stop pawing Eva. And stop trying to be her expert lover. You don't have to please anyone but yourself."

"Just one minute," Arnold shot back incredulously. "I thought Eva wanted me to be *less* selfish, not more. Whose side are you on, anyway?"

"I'm on the side of feelings," I told him. "Yours *and* Eva's. Until you each start focusing on your own feelings, you'll never be happy with one another."

Clearly, Arnold never had been a man who could linger with arousal, so when I saw Eva alone I asked her, "Did you ever wonder why you chose to marry a man who wasn't affectionate?"

"I guess I didn't know what I really wanted then," she replied.

I suspected that there was more to it than that. Eva's background was a perfect complement to Arnold's. The youngest child and only daughter in a large family, she was the apple of her father's eye. She spoke of bouncing on Daddy's knee, having breakfast with him alone in the garden, dancing for him. She said that he was a very affectionate man.

"Affectionate with your mother, too?" I asked.

Eva shrugged, as if I had asked her an indiscreet question.

My guess was that Eva had grown up in a double-message home, too: a seductive father, but an atmosphere of shame surrounding sex. I wondered how she would really respond if Arnold suddenly stopped being a Tough Guy. Three weeks into their Graduated Sensual Exercises, I got my answer.

For the first two weeks Arnold had strenuously resisted feeling anything when it was his turn to lie passively on the bed while Eva caressed him. It was as if every part of his body—except his genitals—were numb. Eva complained that he was hopeless. But that third week, Arnold finally let down his guard and got into the experience; and he said the feelings that flowed through him were fantastic.

"I felt high, in love with Eva and the whole world," he said. "Right up until she brought me down."

It seems the minute they finished the exercise, Eva abruptly asked Arnold if he had made dinner reservations for that night and when he said he had forgotten, she became furious with him, saying that she could not depend on him for anything.

"Funny timing," I said to Eva. "There was Arnold lying beside you, finally loving and sensitive, and you pick that moment to berate him for not being a take-charge guy!"

Eva lowered her eyes in embarrassment. Yes, she was genuinely starved for tender affection, but the moment Arnold gave signs of vulnerability—of not being the strong, fatherlike man she married—she was overcome with anxiety and tried to put a stop to it. Her ambivalence sent Arnold the same double message he had received as a child: *Be sensitive, but be a real man.* Now, in my office, Eva looked over at her husband with a sad smile.

"Sorry," she whispered. "This stuff is a little scary for me, too."

The Sex Fiend and the Eternally Dissatisfied Woman were finally ready to start making love.

Sexier Than Thou

Tough Guys come in a variety of disguises, but the most deceptive is the Pseudo-Romeo. At the beginning of an affair he comes on like a sensualist, a man who can lick and suck and caress for hours on end, but once he becomes involved in an enduring relationship, his sensuality goes out the window. In some cases, his early sensuality turns out to have been a ruse, the physical extension of a seducer's "line." Once he has conquered a woman with his thoughtful, romantic, and unhurried lovemaking, he can dispense with it forevermore and get down to unadulterated genital sex. For him, all the other stuff was just foreplay anyhow—something you got out of the way be*fore* the fun began. In any event, he never really felt very much while he "performed" it.

But for most Pseudo-Romeos, the sensual phase of the relationship is not a ruse at all: indeed, he revels in it for as long as it lasts. Yet it is doomed to end the moment he makes a long-range commitment. Such a man can only permit himself lingering sensual intimacy when he has one foot out of the bed. He is a sensualist only as long as he feels free. In a committed relationship, he is overcome by love anxiety and reverts to typical Tough Guy behavior: doing sex instead of making love.

"What happened to my wonderful Latin lover?" Deidre, a recently married woman, complained to me. "Michael used to be incredible. He could make love for an hour just to my *toe*, for godssake, and I'd tingle all over. Then we got married and he suddenly becomes this sexual robot. Groan, squirt, and that's all," she wrote.

Hers is an all-too-common complaint. In the past, we tended to explain Michael's behavior strictly in terms of the Madonna/Whore complex: once a woman becomes a man's wife, she is sainted, like his mother, and sex is suddenly limited to the "proper" reproductive mode—intercourse, quick and infrequent. But in recent years I have observed a number of married men who are able to indulge in "improper" sexual variations with their wives—including oral-genital sex—*yet who are unable to return to the lingering, sensual lovemaking that they enjoyed before marriage.* Erotic genital experimentation, yes; but intimate affection, no. My guess is this inhibition has more to do with men's fear of powerlessness than it has to do with madonnas and whores. As unattached men, they were not so frightened of being smothered and swallowed up in sensuality: they knew they would eventually go home alone, intact and in control. But as married men, all the old anxieties are called up again: they are frightened of being trapped, losing control, going soft, becoming helpless mamma's boys.

Some Tough Guys deal with these anxieties by becoming aggressively "wild and crazy" lovers.

"I want to taste it all," they tell their partners. "Let's break through all our inhibitions."

I usually admire such adventurousness, especially since so many married men limit themselves to one-note sexuality. But this kind of Tough Guy is not really an adventurer; he is a bully, badgering his partner to "loosen up" and "go with the flow" as he pressures her to try sexual variations she is not quite ready for.

"I always end up feeling guilty because I can't do everything he wants in bed," a young wife told me. "I want to try new things, too, but I have to work up to them. I mean, I'd like a PG-rated love scene before we jump to the X-rated stuff."

Whenever this woman got in bed with her husband, he assumed the role of her teacher and challenger. He was forever chiding her for being an "uptight little girl" who was afraid of sex. Yet when I asked them to try exercises that required this man to linger with arousal, he became more uptight than any virgin bride. This prodigious sexual athlete was terrified of simply lying still and feeling. All his sexual bravado had just been a smoke screen for his own fears. Like Don Juan, he was all control and very little feeling. By becoming the ultimate Pleasure Pusher, by intimidating his wife with his sexier-than-thou superiority, he had not had to face his own terror of intimacy. For him, the PG-rated scenes turned out to be scarier than the X-rated ones.

In Like a Tiger, Out Like a Lamb

Tough Guys are usually dragged into my office kicking and screaming. They let me know right away that the only reason they are here is to satisfy the wife.

"I've got no problem with our sex life," they tell me. *"She does."*

Grudgingly, they submit to my regime as if it were some kind of baptismal fire to make them acceptable to their wives. If they "do" the Sensual Exercises, maybe she will finally stop complaining and come back to bed.

But these exercises work in mysterious ways. A Tough Guy can only go through the motions of caressing and being caressed so many times without letting a little feeling come through. And a little feeling inevitably leads to the desire for more feeling. Gradually, the pleasures of sensual intimacy begin to diminish those peculiarly male anxieties. Lo and behold, he is *not* swallowed up by a wet, lingering kiss—in fact, it feels wonderful. He does *not* become a helpless child when he cuddles in his wife's arms—in fact, he feels more peaceful and secure than he has in years. He does *not* turn into a woman if he lies passively on the bed while she fondles him—in fact, he feels turned on in a more personal way than he has ever felt before. And no, he does *not* lose his potency if he lets his erections come and go during prolonged lovemaking—in fact, he feels perfectly secure in his potency when he moves toward the genital/orgasmic phase of lovemaking.

"My whole life is richer now, not just my love life," said a middle-aged man who had been dragged into my office kicking and screaming only two months earlier. "My food tastes better, my backyard looks prettier, and a long hot bath is my idea of heaven. You see, lying there in bed with my wife touching me all over I finally got the idea: pleasure is everywhere."

 *Chapter 4*

Liberated Women Don't Have Heartthrobs

First it was heart attacks. Statistics showed that women were starting to have more of them, especially women in high-pressure jobs. Doctors told us that it came with the territory of "men's" work: the long hours, the martinis and cigarettes, the relentless stress.

"And controlled emotions," a cardiologist I know added. "In high-performance jobs, you have to stay on top of your emotions all day long or you make yourself vulnerable to the competition. But controlling emotions is bad for your arteries—as bad as steak and ice cream."

It is also bad for your love life. Today, women are having more heart attacks, but fewer heartthrobs. In our struggle for equal power, some of us have controlled our emotions right out of existence. In our terror of being dominated by men—both at the office and at home—some of us have numbed our hearts to *all* loving feelings. Everywhere we look are warnings that if we love too much, we will lose our independence, so we give up on love altogether. And then, like those very men we once scorned, we become cool, out of touch with our feelings, and sexually detached.

"Just as I thought, Dagmar—you're a sexist and an anti-feminist at heart!"

I can hear those women in the front row protesting. *"I suppose next you're going to tell us to become passive, loving little housewives."*

Not at all. But when week after week women come to me lamenting that they "don't feel anything" with their husbands or lovers, I do know that something has gone out of kilter. In the past few years, I have watched the appearance of a whole new set of women's sexual complaints and most of these, like heart attacks, were once reserved primarily for men. If wanting to avoid these "masculine" handicaps makes me a sexist, I plead guilty. And if wanting to combine a capacity for tender affection with a secure sense of independence forces me to lose my feminist status, so be it. I still agree with Freud on the basics: a happy life requires both work *and* love.

The Choirboy/Stud Complex

"I feel positively schizy," Anna K., a prominent art dealer, told me. "At home with Peter and the kids, I'm this model housewife, efficient and proper, and my sex life is about as exciting as a game of Scrabble. But when I've got my professional hat on and I'm traveling, I'm perpetually turned on. I'm always having these mad, erotic fantasies about the man next to me in the airplane or behind me in the elevator. Honestly, I have to stop myself from hitching up my skirt and saying, 'Hey, fella, how about a quickie before we reach the lobby?' All that stops me is guilt, but given the alternative waiting for me at home, that won't stop me for long."

Just two days earlier, Anna had come into my office with her husband in tow, complaining that their sex life was so uninspired it had become an unbearable chore and she rarely reached climax anymore. She described an all-too-typical sexual routine: they only had sex on Saturday nights and rarely kissed or touched on the days in between; these encounters were always limited to "missionary position" sexual intercourse with Peter on top; foreplay never lasted longer than ten minutes and was conducted in the dark in total silence.

Throughout Anna's recap of this Saturday night stupor, Peter, a law professor, continually crossed and uncrossed his arms and legs and stared at the floor. He was clearly ill at ease with his body and with the very subject of sex. His one comment, after he politely waited for his wife to finish, was that he too thought "there was room for improvement." At this point, I had no reason to doubt Anna's assessment that Peter was "not exactly Mr. Frolic in bed."

Now, alone with Anna, I asked her what her sexual experiences before marriage had been like.

"Fabulous!" she said, her large gray eyes brightening. "I had a voracious appetite for hard bodies—particularly, *sweaty* hard bodies—and I indulged it every opportunity I got. I was a regular sexual gourmand. I mean, I actually did do it in an elevator once —the freight elevator of a museum where I was working. I came twice in three floors."

And now she rarely came at all.

"Was this 'quickie' with a man you were seeing regularly at the time?" I asked.

"Hardly!" Anna laughed. "It was with a security guard half my age."

In fact, between college and marriage, most of Anna's sexual encounters had been one-night stands with men who were younger and far less educated than she, men of few words and hard, athletic bodies. Often quickies, these encounters were highly erotic. Until she met Peter when she was twenty-nine, Anna had never dated any one man more than four or five times.

But why had this self-professed sexual athlete chosen to marry such a sexually reticent man?

"Peter's a marvelous man in absolutely every other way,"

Anna told me ingenuously. "He's as smart as they come; he's a wonderful companion and father, steady, supportive of my career—the works. I was the envy of every thirty-year-old girl on my block. I knew the minute I met him that he would make a great husband."

"How could you tell?" I asked. "By the fact that he didn't turn you on?"

"Not fair!" Anna snapped back angrily.

But fairness, we both knew, had nothing to do with it.

🐛

Anna is a classic example of that rapidly spreading syndrome I have dubbed the Choirboy/Stud complex. It is the female version of the Madonna/Whore complex and twenty-five years ago this complaint was as rare as the bald eagle. For women caught in this syndrome, men either make good lovers or good husbands, but *never* both. With their "studs," these women can indulge their every sexual whim, no matter how kinky, *as long as the relationship remains impersonal, as long as they remain in control.* And one way of virtually guaranteeing that it stay impersonal is by only choosing lovers who are perceived as socially "inferior"—particularly younger and less educated men. Good husbands, of course, are precisely the opposite. They are men from "good" backgrounds with solid careers, men who are steady and responsible and, most important, who are *sexually unexciting.* A perfect husband is perfectly safe, which is to say, sexually naive and inhibited. A Choirboy.

In part, the Choirboy/Stud complex is a product of the Sexual Revolution. Only since that taboo-shattering period have women in large numbers admitted to their own powerful sexual desires and had the guts and peer support to act on them. But that alone does not explain why so many women would start dividing the male population into either sex objects or prospective marriage partners. Sexual freedom is not *necessarily* something

41

you practice with a stranger; that, until recently, was traditionally a male distortion.

Anna shared a telling observation with me. In a college psychology course, she had been assigned Nancy Friday's compilation of male sexual fantasies, *Men in Love*, and she had been amazed and appalled by what she found there.

"I was reading about myself!" she told me. "All that typical male stuff, hard-core sex—wanting to get down to it fast and furious and then go home alone—that was *my* idea of sex and always had been. Sex had to do with bodies, not minds and hearts. And the whole purpose of it was to have an orgasm or two or three—what else? Why was this book called **Men** *in Love?* What did that make me?"

It made Anna, like so many other women, terribly confused about her sexual role in this new society. The gender role models she grew up with had offered her two rigidly circumscribed choices: either be a housewife like Mom, passive and dependent in everything, including sex, and ultimately resentful; or be a go-getter professional like Dad, active and independent in everything, including sex. Either/or, nothing in between. There were no role models for being an independent professional woman *and* a sexually active wife at the same time.

No wonder Anna felt schizy. She had "solved" her dilemma by modeling herself after Dad and behaving "like a man" in her independent professional life. (I found it significant that most of her erotic fantasies occurred when she had her professional hat on.) And she had patterned herself after Mom and behaved "like a woman" in her domestic life; by her own description, she was a model housewife—efficient, proper, and virtually sexless. As I quickly discovered, Anna had not only carefully chosen a sexually reticent man for a husband, but she herself had become sexually inhibited in her behavior with him. Their lackluster Saturday nights were as much a result of her own reluctance and passivity as of his. After we had been working together for sev-

eral weeks, Anna admitted to me that she felt "shy" about Peter
seeing her have an orgasm. This from a woman who had come
twice with a stranger in an elevator! Just as men with Madonna/
Whore complexes severely limit their sexuality with their wives
—"I could never do *that* with the mother of my children"—
women with Choirboy/Stud complexes are passive and unre-
sponsive in bed with their husbands. But inevitably such women
end up frustrated and, like Anna, terrified that they will become
unfaithful.

What were Anna's options?

She did not want to even consider divorce. She loved Peter and
family life too much for that. The idea of being single again
made her unbearably sad. And, to her credit, she already understood that at this point she would be sexually numb with *whom-
ever* she might end up with if she remarried.

Another option would be for her to lead the same kind of
double life that many men have traditionally led: have erotic sex
outside the home with impersonal lovers while continuing to
have unfeeling sex inside the home with her spouse. In its way,
this has worked for centuries in some cultures—mistresses and
whores are for sexual fun while wives are for home life and as
little sex as you can get away with. Indeed, I have spoken to
several women who have co-opted this traditionally male manner of playing out the Madonna/Whore complex. They glide
easily from a peck on the cheek with the father of their children
to a hot embrace with their hotel lover. Typically, these are
women who "have it all" by pigeonholing everything—especially people—according to their own needs. They socialize with
certain friends for networking and other friends for relaxing and
gossiping, certain friends for family outings, others for formal
affairs. The problem, of course, is that one can end up feeling
fragmented and superficial. For Anna, this solution would have
been an extension of the life she was already leading; now she

would be acting out her sexual fantasies. But again, she did not believe she could handle it.

"Maybe I'm still not completely liberated," she said to me, "but if fooling around ever became a steady thing for me, I think I'd have trouble coming home to the kids. I'd feel like a fraud with them."

And so Anna was left with the option that had brought her into my office in the first place: trying to have a satisfying love life with her husband.

"I'd be lying if I assured you that with a little encouragement Peter will turn into one of your spontaneous studs before your very eyes," I told Anna. "Yet who knows? There might be a sensual Superman lurking behind that mild-mannered Clark Kent exterior."

But her job, I said, was to forget about Peter's inhibitions altogether and concentrate on her own. At this point, Anna was the female equivalent of a Tough Guy: she was fearful of *intimate lovemaking* with either Stud or Choirboy. With her erotic lovers, she had avoided intimacy by doing sex; with her husband, she avoided intimacy by doing very little at all. Ultimately, her fear of lingering with affection and arousal was identical to the Tough Guy's fear: she was afraid of turning into a "woman": *the totally dependent and passive kind of woman her mother was and ultimately resented being.* She would become "impotent" as a forceful and independent career woman. She would succumb to pointless pleasure and never be in control of her life again.

Often, when a Choirboy does begin to respond to the Sensual Exercises, his wife backs away immediately. This is not what she had bargained for when she chose this shy and awkward guy. One reticent husband I know suddenly decided that he wanted to fondle his wife's naked body *on the kitchen table* "like a huge banquet." His wife, a woman who frequently had wild sexual adventures with younger men, was horrified when her husband fell out of his expected role. "Help! He's turned kinky on me," she said to me. I told her that she was afraid she might get turned on by it.

Anna's husband, Peter, never did become the Mr. Frolic of her dreams—which probably would have overwhelmed her anyway. Peter remained a shy, if tender, lover. Yet after months of Sensual Exercises, Anna found she was beginning to take pleasure in his body even if it wasn't a stranger's "hard" body. And as she learned to linger with arousal, she found that having orgasms with him ceased to be a problem. They began touching and kissing each other more casually and making love more frequently. Anna still has fantasies in elevators—all the time, in fact—but she sees them less as real temptations or threats to her marriage.

"I'll always miss the wild stuff, I guess," she told me recently. "But there's a sweetness in making love with Peter that I never had before. Is it just a compromise? Maybe. But it sure feels better being one loving person than being two desperate people."

The Long and the Short of It

I admit it. No woman has actually come into my office and declared, "I come too soon!"

That's strictly a man's complaint, although it's usually his wife who does the complaining. No, *women* complain that they take *too long* to reach orgasm, that by the time they are finally getting close, he's done, exhausted.

Still, I have begun to see women's "Premature Orgasms" as a growing problem among educated, hard-working women. But it was women's complaints of *unsatisfying* orgasms that gave me my first clue that an increasing number of them were coming too soon. They arrived in my office lamenting that the thrill was gone, that their orgasms had "dimmed out." And others arrived wondering if they were having orgasms at all—they weren't sure. In a surprising number of these cases, I discovered that the women were rushing to orgasms in a matter of only a few minutes, sometimes even in seconds. Here we have yet another typically masculine symptom which some women have adopted so that they can cut arousal short—so that they can do sex instead of making love.

Of course, there is an obvious difference between a man's premature ejaculation and a woman's premature orgasm. When a man comes, he loses his erection; thus, when he comes too quickly, his partner is deprived of her orgasm—at least from intercourse. When a woman comes, she is physically able to continue having intercourse until her partner reaches orgasm—with some notable exceptions, as we will see.

But for both women and men, premature orgasms serve the same purpose: it permits them to avoid the terrors and wonders of intimate sensuality. It allows them to get the whole thing over with a neat ending, that sexual punctuation mark, orgasm. Women with this symptom not only miss out on sensuality, but they have less powerful and less satisfying orgasms.

Consider Gabby F. whose husband, Roland, actually did complain that she came too soon. I offer their story not because it is typical in its particulars—it is, in fact, rather unusual—but because it illustrates the *general* problem of female premature orgasm quite vividly.

At sixty-two, Roland was chairman of a small but prestigious investment firm. Three years earlier, his wife of over thirty-five years had died; a year later, he had married Gabby, the thirty-two-year-old senior vice president of his company. An admittedly "old-fashioned" gentleman, Roland had not wanted to have sexual relations with Gabby until after they were married. He was in for a tremendous disappointment.

The only other woman with whom Roland had ever made love was his first wife and with her he had enjoyed an unusually sensual relationship. They had made love frequently—three or four times a week well into their fifties—but more to the point, they usually spent hours at it, including a good long period after intercourse began. Despite his formal manner and aristocratic bearing, Roland was an inveterate sensualist. Unfortunately, he had made the assumption that Gabby was one, too.

Indeed, Gabby's voluptuous beauty, provocative way of dressing, and flirtatious manner might have led any man to believe that she was a woman with a large sexual appetite. By her own estimation, she had a "healthy" capacity for sex. She had had lovers since she was sixteen and many of them, she assured me, had complimented her on her sexual ease.

"I never had any trouble having orgasms the way lots of other young women I knew did," she told me. "I could always come on a dime. I remember, I used to be able to bring myself off in seconds just by squeezing my legs together in the back of the school bus."

But "coming on a dime" was precisely what had made their love life disastrous, according to Roland. He had expected to enjoy the same kind of lingering lovemaking with Gabby as he had with his first wife. In fact, he had secretly hoped it would be even more sensuous with this voluptuous younger woman "at the peak of her sexual powers." Yet not only did Gabby come within minutes after intercourse began, but four or five minutes afterward she would complain of vaginal dryness and discomfort and would insist that he withdraw. Unfulfilled, he would masturbate to orgasm.

"I've never known a man to take so long to come," she complained to me. "If he had his way, he'd last all night. I certainly have always thought of sex as a natural function, but for him it's a fetish."

She admitted that Roland's age and gentlemanly manner had led her to expect sex to play a relatively small role in their married life. Clearly, that was also what she had hoped for.

Was Roland taking too long to come? Was he having what is

called in the psychiatric literature "retarded ejaculations"? Or was Gabby coming too soon? Was she having what I call "premature orgasms"?

Any categorizing of "too long" or "too short" is ultimately a judgment of *generally* desired behavior. And frequently this judgment reflects an unspoken gender bias. A man who comes within one minute after insertion is usually described negatively as a "premature ejaculator," whereas a woman who comes within one minute after insertion is often described positively as "easily orgasmic." And a woman who takes over an hour after insertion to reach orgasm is considered dysfunctional, whereas the equivalent man is usually considered as having admirable sexual endurance. The liberal solution to this dilemma would be to admit that these concepts are relative to specific individuals and to only use them that way. Thus, all we would be able to say is that Gabby comes too soon *for* Roland and that Roland takes too long to come *for* Gabby.

But I am not happy with that way of thinking either. My bias will come as no surprise to anyone. For me, a man *or* woman comes too soon if he or she is rushing the experience in order to avoid sensual intimacy—that is, if it is in the service of doing sex instead of making love. And likewise, a man *or* woman takes too long to come if he or she is withholding feeling in order to avoid anxiety associated with sensual intimacy—again, if it is in the service of doing sex instead of making love. And that, for me, is the long and the short of it.

For example, I believe a man has a problem with retarded ejaculation if I see that he is driven by a need to always be in control of sex and can never allow himself the pleasures of being passive with his partner. He takes an hour to come (or never comes at all) because he is only able to experience sex as an achievement akin to an athletic competition. He is a Star Lover and his partner is his audience. For him, sex is all mastery and no enjoyment because he is terrified of being vulnerable. And I think he has a problem. But in my estimation, Roland was not taking so long to come because he wanted to dominate Gabby; rather, I believe he truly wanted them both to enjoy the kind of lingering sensuality and intimacy he had enjoyed with his first wife. Roland's problem was his impatience and his insensitivity to Gabby's fears and vulnerabilities.

Similarly, I consider a woman "easily orgasmic" if I see that she can flow from her quick orgasm to other sensual experiences and then perhaps to another, more powerful orgasm. But if I have clues that her one-minute orgasm is a way of short-circuiting feelings, a way to get the whole business over with, then I believe she has a problem that is getting in the way of her enjoyment of lovemaking. I had a number of such clues from Gabby. The very vocabulary she used to describe sex—"a natural function"—sounded more like it applied to bathroom behavior than to romantic encounters. When I grew up in Sweden, people frequently talked about sex in such prosaic, mechanical terms and there, too, it reflected a distinctly antiromantic attitude. Another clue was Gabby's description of her rapid-fire orgasms on the bus when she was a schoolgirl. Many of the women I see who complain of having "dim" orgasms experienced their first orgasms by secretly flexing their thighs in this way. Childhood masturbation is a joy I would not want anyone to miss; for a young girl, in particular, it can be a liberating experience which opens her up to her capacity for sensual pleasure. But, just as for a boy, a girl's routine of superquick, clandestine masturbation—to avoid getting "caught" and to avoid facing guilt—can be early training in anxious nonsensual, purely genital sex and in weak, unfulfilling orgasms.

Gabby's postorgastic vaginal dryness and consequent soreness offered me the most telling clue. I do not want to get into any mind/body arguments here; I am well aware that many sexual problems are caused by physical incapacities and that is why I always require patients with dysfunctions to be checked out by

49

their urologists or gynecologists. I am also aware that some women's vaginal walls do not lubricate adequately for organic reasons: but Gabby had no trouble lubricating *prior* to her orgasm: then, in fact, she lubricated quickly and copiously. It was only *after* orgasm that she became so dry she could not tolerate intercourse and my guess was that it was for psychogenic reasons; from somewhere deep inside her psyche she told her sexual parts to dry up and shut down. My guess turned out to be right.

As I got to know more about Gabby, I discovered that she was very much the female equivalent of a premature ejaculator. She was deeply involved in a demanding and highly competitive career. She viewed most everything in her life in terms of goals and the most efficient way to reach them. She could never just "hang out," and she had little tolerance for pointless pleasure. By only indulging in one-minute sex, she remained in control, undistracted from her goals. And she was so sexually attractive and "accomplished" in sexual techniques that she had been able to bring virtually all her previous lovers to orgasms as quickly as she came herself. These, ostensibly, were the men who had complimented her on her sexual ease: she came in a minute, they came in a minute—everybody could get back to business. I was reminded of the Faye Dunaway character in the movie *Network* who talked excitedly about new programming concepts while she straddled her lover, William Holden: she barely missed a beat in her pitch as she reached orgasm.

On a hunch, I asked Gabby if she had ever felt discriminated against because of her beauty.

"You bet I have!" she replied, with more than a touch of bitterness in her voice. It seemed that ever since she was a little girl, Gabby's parents and teachers had focused exclusively on her physical attributes without ever giving her intelligence its due. She was the pretty one; her brother was the smart one. Like so many bright young girls of her generation, Gabby justifiably felt exploited and demeaned by this appraisal. Early on, she resolved to prove that she was more than just a pretty face, and she had succeeded fabulously.

"I won't deny that my looks opened a door or two," she told me, "but once I was inside that door, I knew my stuff as well as any other M.B.A. Instead of being exploited for my attractiveness, I used it to prove my real capabilities."

But like so many women and men who capitalize on their sexual attractiveness to gain an audience or power, Gabby had sacrificed her sexual feelings. To "give in" to those sexual feelings was tantamount to losing the very power her sexual attractiveness had gained her. She would be back to square one, the beautiful but helpless little girl. For her, coming "on a dime" was roughly the same as not coming at all: it kept her from being subjugated by feelings.

By the time Roland and Gabby reached my office, they were both angry. Roland felt deeply frustrated by their unsatisfactory sex, and he felt deceived by Gabby's apparent sexiness. Gabby, on the other hand, was offended by the way Roland constantly compared her to his first wife, and she felt bullied by his sexual demands. It took months of argument, discussion, separate sessions, and Graduated Sensual Exercises for these two to start edging toward each other. Roland had to learn to see Gabby as an individual and not as a replica of his first wife; he had to learn to appreciate her own desires and fears, whatever he had once expected from her. And Gabby had to learn that pleasure and power do not necessarily exclude one another: that she could feel secure in the boardroom *and* in bed. To get her to that point, I first worked with her in a women's group where she learned to masturbate slowly, lingering with arousal, letting it build, rather than rushing to orgasm. In time Gabby discovered that she could indulge in a sensual hour or two with her husband without feeling exploited, controlled, or demeaned, and in the process she found that she was coming less and less quickly and that she was not drying up between her several increasingly powerful and delightful orgasms.

Superwoman Sucks Her Thumb

Years ago, I frequently saw passive, "Little Girl" housewives who found sex ugly and scary. Often, they reported sexual phobias, such as a fear of suffocating during intercourse. All these women wanted from their husbands were paternal hugs and little dry kisses, comfort not sensuality. Typically, such women did not have careers and did not consider themselves men's equals. The only way they could learn how to enjoy mature lovemaking was by first learning how to be more assertive and self-respecting. Optimist that I am, I was confident that the Women's Movement would spell the end of this particular syndrome.

It was not to be. Today, I am still seeing women with Little Girl sexual phobias—except now these women are doctors and lawyers, producers and investment bankers. They are unarguably the equal of any man I know in the grown-up world and certainly few of them lack for assertiveness on the job. But at home with their husbands, they are sexually insecure and frightened and desperately in need of sexless paternal comforting. For their husbands, it is confusing to say the least. They never suspected that Superwoman sucked her thumb.

I saw Martha W. on television long before she appeared in my office with her husband, Mark. Martha is a witty, aggressive, and very powerful member of the Washington TV press corps known for "beating" a story out of the most reluctant government official. Mark, a congressional press secretary, readily admits that he fell in love with Martha when he saw her "working over the President" at a press conference.

"I'd never seen such *chutzpah* and energy in all of Washington," he told me. "She knocked me out."

But after only two years of marriage, Mark was seeing quite a different person at home.

"She can barely get through dinner without getting weepy about something," Mark said. "Usually it's about somebody who hurt her feelings at the studio or some interview she thinks she's totally unprepared for, but she just starts falling apart in front of me. And I've got to get up and lead her by the hand to the couch and stroke her hair and tell her that everything's going to be all right. 'Uhm, uhm, baby.' I usually end up singing her a lullaby."

On one night in particular, Mark was struck by the extreme contrast between his wife's two personas.

"Martha was lying on the couch with her head in my lap sniffling again when all of a sudden I saw her on the TV making mincemeat of somebody from the State Department on the seven-o'clock news." Mark shook his head. "There she was, the Formidable Martha, the one I'd fallen in love with, but I could barely hear her over the sobs of the Poor Little Martha I was married to."

"So now you know the truth, I'm the Wizard of Oz," Martha responded with bittersweet irony. "I'm not merely the person you see on TV, I'm human, too, with all kinds of feelings including insecurities. And for the first time in my adult life I thought I had somebody I could share these feelings with, somebody I could trust so much I could finally let my guard down. Except I was wrong. Now you're telling me to stop."

"No, you're the one who's always telling *me* to stop!" Mark countered angrily. "Every time I want to make love to you!"

"I can't help it!" Martha wailed. "It hurts!"

Here, then, was the crux of the matter. In their two years of marriage, Martha and Mark had made love less than a dozen times because the very prospect of sex made Martha increasingly anxious and frightened. She said that it hurt, although her gynecologist could find no organic reason why intercourse should be painful for her. She said she was too exhausted for sex, although she remained one of the most energetic reporters in Washington. Then she developed that classic Little Girl phobia: she said that she literally felt she was suffocating when Mark lay on top of her. Each one of these symptoms was new for her, only developing *after* she got married.

Mark said he felt cheated. Not only had he expected Martha to remain a stimulating conversationalist at the dinner table, but he claimed that he had expected her to remain an active grown-up lover in bed.

"I could have just as well married my nineteen-year-old secretary," he moaned. "At least she would have cooked dinner before she fell apart."

Martha, like women in the Choirboy/Stud syndrome, had parceled her life into two parts: in her professional life, she was one person, dynamic and independent; and at home, she was another person, passive and dependent. Yet these roles played out with a new variation. With her professional hat on, Martha's energies were focused exclusively on her job, not on sexual fantasies or affairs. But at home with the "man of the house" she regressed to her earliest female model. "Daddy's little girl"—insecure, frightened of criticism, and terrified of sex. Ironically, the only kinds of physical contact she felt comfortable with—rocking and petting and stroking—are a significant part of what I find lacking in most relationships. These tendernesses are what the Tough Guys of the world—both male and female—need so badly. But Martha was missing the other half of lovemaking. While she yearned to be stroked, she was incapable of stroking her husband back because then she would lose her status as a dependent and needy little girl. But most significantly, while she could linger with affection, she could not move from it into sexual arousal. One or another of her phobias always prevented that from happening.

Frightened, needy, and inflexible, Martha was far from able to enjoy mature lovemaking.

But, as we soon found out, so was Mark. Once again, the Sensual Exercises smoked out an Inhibited Lover posing as a Pleasure Pusher. When it was Mark's turn to lie passively on the bed while Martha caressed him, he could not relax for a moment. He relentlessly directed and criticized her every movement.

"Her touch was so timid, I could barely feel it," he complained in my office after over a month of these exercises, during which Martha had become increasingly active and giving.

"No, the reason you couldn't feel anything is because you're unwilling to give up any control," I said to him. "You see, now that Martha isn't being such a Little Girl anymore, you've got to give up being Big Daddy."

Although Mark had *claimed* to be totally surprised when the formidable Martha whom he married turned out to be a thumbsucker at home, my guess is that his male radar had detected the dependent Little Girl hidden inside her long before the wedding. Like many "liberated" men I've seen these past few years, Mark actually wanted his woman both ways: he wanted her aggressive and accomplished in the public world (the yuppie equivalent of a showgirl on his arm), but he really wanted her dependent and unthreatening at home.

In the end, it was Martha who was able to grow up, to overcome her phobias and to merge comforting affection with sensual lovemaking. But Mark, sadly, never could accept this less needy and more sexually active Martha. He felt threatened by what he saw as her new demands on him; remarkably, he even said that he was beginning to feel suffocated by her in bed. Finally, he refused to continue with therapy. Several months later, they separated.

"I'm sad, of course," Martha told me on the phone recently. "But I know the only way the marriage could have lasted is if neither of us changed. And I know I didn't really want to be a frightened little-girl wife for the rest of my life. No blame, as the *I Ching* says. It will be better next time."

Men Who Need Stroking and the Women Who Jump Them

If Mark had been able to stick with the Sensual Exercises long enough to overcome his anxieties about losing control, he would have discovered the joys of being made love to—a rare treat for most men. One of the most gratifying aspects of my work is hearing men report how much they enjoy this newfound pleasure.

"I had no idea what I was missing until I finally just gave up, lay perfectly still, and let [her] stroke me," one husband told me. "What an incredible feeling! It was like I'd been deprived of this wonderful stuff my whole life."

Indeed, most men *are* deprived of tender affection from the time they are young boys. While their sisters are getting hugs and loving caresses, they are getting manly pats on the shoulder or squeezes on the back of the neck. Most men grow to adulthood without realizing how much they hunger for affection—for the relaxed intimacy and comfort it could afford them. But once they are able to accept it, they revel in it.

That's the good news. The sad news is that a great number of contemporary women are unable to give their men the affection they want. Women with the Choirboy/Stud complex are totally focused on genital sex to the exclusion of tender sensuality. Likewise, women who are prematurely orgasmic cut out affection by skipping to the end point of sex. And thumb-sucking Superwomen such as Martha can *take* affection all day long—as long as it does not lead to erotic sex and as long as they do not have to give any affection in return. In one respect, these liberated women are exactly like our sisters from an earlier era—the virginal "nice girls," the timid "little girls," and the teasing "coquettes": they are all frightened of intimate lovemaking.

But it takes two to tangle. Whom we choose to marry usually reflects our sexual inhibitions more than it reflects our sexual ambitions. Tough Guys who can't smooch marry Liberated Women who don't have heartthrobs and after a while, neither of them is very satisfied. Rigid, limiting roles have to be broken out of together.

It begins with a touch, a lingering, sensual touch.

❧ Chapter 5

The World's Oldest Deal: Trading Sex for Love and Vice Versa ❧

Sex is for men and Love is for women. This is the premise of the oldest trade-off in history: Marriage.

If the above sounds like a doctrine from ancient history, think again. Even stated that baldly, it wouldn't have shocked many of our mothers and grandmothers. I know scores of women who remember scenes of Mother reluctantly traipsing upstairs to the bedroom with a sigh, a shrug, maybe even a joke which said, "Ho hum, it's time to perform my conjugal duties. It's time to *do* Papa."

Clearly, Mother did not endure Papa's regularly scheduled pokes because it gave her any pleasure. She did it because it was part of their "deal." She had no confusion about that either: he gave her a home, a family, security, respectability—in short, the elements she construed as "love." And that entitled Poppa to "scratch his little itch" with her twice a week. What's more, it was Mother's way of guaranteeing that he wouldn't go somewhere else to take care of his itch.

Most of my teenage friends were scandalized by the deal their mothers had made.

"Marriage is just legalized prostitution," one of my girlfriends used to cry in disgust. That girl swore to me that she would never make a deal like that, even if it meant remaining single for her entire life. She was not going to cheapen herself or her dreams of true love in that way. But that girl did get married less than five years later, as did most of the rest of us.

Did we modern women—women with education, professions, self-knowledge, and self-esteem—establish marriages free of any such deals?

Not all of us. I am sad to say that in my opinion bartering sex for love and vice versa is still often the name of the game. Let's consider some facts:

In the vast majority of modern marriages, sex continues to be practiced by *both* partners as if it were *primarily for men*—his prerogative, not hers. There is no better indication of this than the statistics on who most frequently initiates sex in marriage; as we coast into the last year of the Decade of the Woman, four couples out of five still say it's the *husband.* At a cocktail party or even at the office, this husband may argue eloquently (and sincerely) for equality of the sexes, but chances are that under the covers, he is still the one who slips his hand onto her belly and says, "Hey, it's been over a week now, hon, hasn't it?"

As for the other side of the ledger, it appears that love and affection are still most frequently seen by *both* partners as *primarily for women.* Ask Ann Landers. A few years back the famed columnist ran a survey on what wives wanted most from their husbands and, believe me, the answer was *not* multiple orgasms. No, women wanted sweet nothings whispered in their ears, presents of flowers and bonbons, and above all, women said that they wanted to be cuddled. And cuddling was enough, thank you. In fact, a good number of the respondents said that they would be more than willing to sacrifice one weekly roll in the hay for one tender embrace. In short, they would willingly trade sex for love. I doubt if one man in a hundred would admit to wanting to make the same sacrifice.

So it appears that the old premise is still in place—not ancient history after all. The time-honored deal still seems ready to be struck. Yet in this age of "enlightenment" between the sexes, things get trickier, deals get murkier. Especially now that we have lived through the Sexual Revolution and the female orgasm has to be put in the balance.

"Whose Orgasm Is It, Anyway?"

The moment Dina and Louis F. entered my office, Dina informed me with a gracious smile that she was only here for her husband's sake. It was all his idea, this pretty, immaculately dressed and coiffed office manager told me. *He* was the one who had made the appointment; *he* was the one who was upset.

I asked Louis, a postal clerk, why he was upset.

"It's Dina," he answered quietly. "She doesn't have orgasms."

So Dina was here for Louis's sake and he was here for hers. On the surface, at least, they appeared to be quite an altruistic pair.

"I really don't know why Louis is making such a big thing out of it," Dina went on brightly. "I think we have a very satisfying relationship. I mean, I believe one can be perfectly happy without having to have a, you know, orgasm."

When she uttered the word "orgasm," Dina raised one eyebrow and offered a half-smile as if the very idea of having an orgasm was beneath her. She seemed to be saying, "I'm not one of those tawdry women."

I looked at Louis who was shaking his head slowly.

"Well, if Dina's not bothered by not having an orgasm, why should you be?" I asked him.

"It's just not right," he sputtered, obviously holding back a raft of anger. "It's just not natural."

"You mean, you think she's deliberately holding back on you," I said.

Louis flushed and Dina suddenly began coughing uncontrollably. I seemed to have touched a sensitive spot. Apparently it was not just mutual good will we were dealing with here after all.

The notion that every woman not only is capable of having an orgasm, but is *entitled* to one, is a relatively new idea. A generation or two ago, it was generally assumed that only the rare female had orgasms and she had them infrequently. Indeed, many doctors assumed that there was a *physical* reason for this. Some theories even went so far as to say that the human female had physically evolved *beyond* orgasm, that since it was no longer required for the Darwinian purpose of reproducing the species, the female nervous system had started to phase it out. Thus, most women assumed that they probably could not have orgasms and were not actively disappointed when their assumption turned out to be true. They may have felt frustrated, but they figured it was just their lot in life. No doubt about it, sex was for men. We can be pretty sure that when Mother traipsed reluctantly up the stairs to *do* Papa, she really was not thinking about any erotic ecstasy of her own; if she anticipated any pleasure at all, it was the pleasure of hugs and kisses—of love and affection.

But then in the 1950s and 1960s all that began to change. *Mirabile dictu,* sex researchers announced that women *could* have orgasms—every one of them. Sex was democratic after all. Maybe not all women could have vaginal orgasms every time, but certainly clitoral orgasms. So even if a woman did not have an orgasm in intercourse, she could count on having one from manual or oral stimulation. It was a giant step forward for woman's equality—literally, for *sexual* equality. Certainly this would put an end to bartering sex for love in marriage. Men and women could provide *each other* with sexual pleasure. It was a time for rejoicing.

But not everyone was cheering. Suddenly, both women and

men were faced with a whole new set of sexual expectations, sexual demands, and sexual frustrations. The female orgasm—the big "O"—instantly became a challenge and a test. What should have been pure sexual joy very quickly became the highest stake in sexual politics.

Women were suddenly thinking, "If I don't have an orgasm, I'm a failure." And, of course, that pressure alone was enough to keep many of them from even coming close to climaxing.

At the same time, their husbands and lovers were thinking, "If she doesn't have an orgasm, *I'm* a failure." They seized upon the female orgasm as an acid test of whether or not they were good lovers, as the definitive answer to that eternally haunting male question.

What joyous lovemaking!

From bedrooms all around the world came a male chorus of, "Was it good for you, too?"

At first the question was asked timidly, worriedly. Did I ring the bell? Did I make the grade? Did I last long enough? Oh God, maybe I'm doing it wrong.

If the woman answered unequivocally, yes, she did have an orgasm, the man was immensely pleased and relieved. He had gotten his reward. *He* had made her come.

Right then and there resentments developed.

"My husband always gets this smug look on his face when he knows I've come," one woman told me. "It's like he's done this wonderful thing *all by himself* and I'm supposed to be terribly grateful to him for being such a stud. That look on his mug has nothing to do with love, let me tell you."

But if the woman answered, no, she had *not* come, her lover was crestfallen. He felt like a failure and, as people are wont to do when they feel like failures, he took it out on the person closest at hand. The next time he asked, "Was it good for you, too?" there was an undertone of desperation and anger in his voice.

It is often at this point that some women begin to fake orgasms. What a sad and strange deception this is when you really think about it: at the climax of this supposedly most intimate of acts *to lie about what you feel.* To me, this lie is the absolute opposite of intimacy. And yet a great many women who have had difficulty reaching orgasm feel compelled to go through this charade every time they engage in intercourse with their husbands or lovers.

"Look, I know it's a silly deception," one woman told me. "But it sure beats the hell out of the alternative which is having him mope around for the rest of the week. Nobody's hurt, really, and it makes him feel better."

Ah yes, altruism again. She is making her husband a "gift" of her fraudulent orgasm.

Other women sounded less charitable when they told me why they put on this bedroom high drama of crescendoing moans and beatific smiles. (Inspired as they are by Hollywood's version of sexual ecstasy, I am sure that faked orgasms are infinitely more glamorous to behold than the genuine article.)

"I do it to keep him off my back," one of these women said to me. "Otherwise he'd want to go at it every spare moment until he finally hit the jackpot. I suppose that could be fun if it weren't such a joyless pursuit."

This woman was on her way to understanding who finally gets faked out in a faked orgasm: herself. Faking an orgasm is the ultimate act of focusing on your partner's feelings and not on your own feelings; it virtually guarantees that you will not feel anything yourself. Remarkably, once several women in my groups stopped faking orgasms they discovered that they had actually been having orgasms all along. They had been so involved in putting on a good show that they denied the genuine feelings behind the show.

There are even some women who feel pressured to dramatize

the orgasms they are having in order to placate a husband who insists that she is not demonstrative enough.

"I usually hold my breath just as I'm starting to climax," one wife told me. "But my husband kept complaining that I wasn't having real powerful orgasms so I started throwing in a few moans and groans. Now's he's happier, but I get so caught up in my act that I sometimes lose it."

The peril of show business is that the real feeling can get lost. I used to say that faking an orgasm is a sure way not to have one, but in recent years I discovered an important exception to this rule. Some women in my preorgasmic groups are so terrified of appearing too sexual (and hence, tawdry), that they need "practice" in hearing themselves moan, in sucking in their breath and rolling their eyes. In short, they need to rehearse having an orgasm a few times in order to overcome their inhibitions about how they look. They need to get the "feel" of being that wild. Only then can they allow themselves to focus on the feelings that will let them enjoy an orgasm.

But whether female orgasms were faked, denied, or simply not there, the new emphasis on the big "O" frequently just made the trade-offs in a marriage more complicated. Men were bartering for ego, women were bartering for peace. And somewhere in the transaction mutual intimate feelings got lost once again.

"I Love You . . . (Pause) . . . Say Something, Damn It!"

"This never happened with anyone else," Louis immediately announced to me when I saw him alone. And then, as many husbands and lovers of preorgasmic women had done before him, Louis produced his list of all the women he had slept with who not only had orgasms, but had multiple orgasms. A muscular man in his mid-thirties with sensitive-looking eyes, Louis seemed to be someone who put a lot of effort into trying to appear tougher and more macho than he actually felt. I was not at all surprised when he told me that he had been the youngest of four brothers, the one who always had to keep up with the others. Right now, Louis wanted me to know for certain that there was nothing wrong with his "equipment," that he was perfectly adequate at doing sex.

"But after all those women, you chose to marry Dina, the one who *didn't* have orgasms with you," I said, after he had run through his list. "Maybe we ought to start by looking into the reasons why you chose her."

Louis replied that Dina was quite wonderful in every other way: she was superefficient at her job, a gracious hostess, a good mother, a consummate homemaker. He also said that she was a very thoughtful wife who, for example, always had dinner waiting for him when he came home. It was clear to me that Louis was in awe of his wife. In his opinion, Dina's job was more prestigious than his, her social skills more refined. Obviously Louis thought of himself as having married up and Dina was on a pedestal. But at the same time, the Dina he was describing sounded like a regular geisha: a woman devoted to the art of pleasing her man without daring to really please herself.

I asked Louis if Dina ever initiated sex with him and he replied no, in a tone that showed he thought the idea was fairly preposterous. I asked him if Dina ever refused to have sex when he initiated it and he said never, although he did say that she always made him wait until she was absolutely sure the children were asleep, which sometimes meant delaying sex until quite late at night. Then, he complained, she usually decided that the bedroom needed to be cleaned up and finally, she devoted a great deal of time to preparing herself—showering, powdering, and perfuming her body, combing her hair, dressing in a frilly nightgown. Once in bed, he said, she liked to talk quietly for a while and then, just before they started, she always said, "I love you."

"And you always say the same thing back to her?" I asked.

"Yes."

"Even if you don't feel like it?"

Louis hesitated, then nodded yes.

The ritual of responsively saying "I love you" and "I love you, too" before sex can begin has a long history which dates back to the days when bartering sex for love was more explicit. A woman needed a declaration of love before she could allow sex because she needed assurance that her lover would stay around to support the results of sex—namely, children. It was not simply an emotional need she wanted fulfilled, it was a practical need. "Yes, I want to have your children," she was saying, "but I have to know that you want these children, too. Promise me you'll help me care for them. . . . Tell me that you love me."

Remnants of this primal behavior linger on. Many middle-aged men I know remember that as pre–Sexual Revolution teenagers they learned that the only way to get into a girl's cardigan was through sweet talk.

"The rule of the game was that a girl wouldn't 'put out' unless you convinced her that you truly cared for her," one of these men explained to me. "So we all developed soulful looks in our eyes and a line of romantic poesy straight out of Hallmark cards all for the express purpose of fondling a bare breast. God forbid that the girl should do it simply because she felt turned on, too."

A cliché of 1950s movies was a demure young thing pushing her panting beau away and saying to him, "You don't want me just for sex, do you?" which he would deny vehemently, finally coming up with proof positive of his decent intentions in the form of his high school ring—the symbol of love. He wanted sex, all right, but he knew the going price for it.

Although the times have changed, I sometimes wonder if the differences are only stylistic. Even at the end of the eighties, there are still many women like Dina who need to hear those three little words before they can proceed with sexual contact. Perhaps most of them don't compel their men to make that declaration on cue just before bedtime, but the requirement is still there.

I've always thought that the need to say "I love you, too" immediately after your partner says "I love you" was a pretty grim business. A case in point is the following episode described to me by a young husband, Steven.

"Beth [his wife] and I were out for a drive in the country having a perfectly lovely time when suddenly she gave me a kiss and said, 'I love you.' Terrific. Always glad to hear it. But it just so happened that at that particular moment I didn't feel the urge to say it back. I figured we were both in such great moods, it didn't matter. *Wrong!* Beth kept staring at me with this expression of, 'Well, aren't you going to say anything?' on her face and pretty soon she was pouting and wouldn't talk to me at all. I leaned over to kiss her but she turned away. No kiss for me. I hadn't played by the rules."

This woman's need for reassurance had the effect of turning the most intimate of expressions into polite behavior, making the words "I love you" no different from "Thank you," "Excuse me," or "Have a nice day." Etiquette dictates that you *must* say it even if you don't really feel it. Unhappily, when saying "I love you" becomes a prerequisite for having sex, those words become devoid of their original emotional power. In fact, when a man trades those words for sex—even as part of a harmless ritual, as Louis did—he is participating in the male equivalent of a woman's faked orgasm. By saying "I love you" *on order,* he risks never genuinely experiencing the intimate feelings behind those words.

"Just a second, Dagmar!" I hear that woman in the back row pro-

testing again. *"All we are trying to do is to get a little love back into our sex lives. You, of all people, can hardly blame us for that."*

I don't blame you for a moment; my whole aim is to see love and sex joined in a relationship. But any attempt to *trade one for the other* is bound to keep love and sex separate. And the end result of that is *two* lonely and frustrated people.

Louis's sexual experiences with his wife as he described them to me sounded particularly lonely. Once the protocol "I love you"s were out of the way, Dina got swiftly down to business. She reached for Louis's penis, manipulated it to erection—again she sounded like an expert geisha to me—then guided it inside her as she slipped a pillow under her buttocks. In spite of all this efficiency, Louis managed to last quite long before coming, and afterward, even after all these years, he frequently tortured them both by asking the perennial question: *"Was it good for you, too?"*

According to Louis, Dina would never pretend that she'd had an orgasm. She would reply to Louis, "It doesn't matter, darling. It will happen when it happens. Anyhow, it just makes me feel good to know that it was so good for you."

I have it on good authority that this kind of response is enough to drive most men right up the wall. I am sure that in her way Dina was being sincere, but her answer flirts dangerously close to martyrdom. Louis admitted that there was something about her response that always made him feel terrible, although at this point he could not say exactly why that was.

It seemed to me that Dina was probably conveying a number of messages to Louis with her answer. First, by saying that "it didn't matter," she was suggesting that she was "above" orgasms and that Louis, as a male who needed sex and was merely carnal, was beneath her. The way Louis had put Dina on a pedestal, he was all too willing to buy this attitude, even if he was beginning to resent it. But the most dangerous part of this message is that it reenforced the basic feeling Louis had about all of their sex life: *that he was doing it all alone.*

Next, Dina's line that "it will happen when it happens" sounded to me like a subtle prod for him to keep trying to make her have an orgasm. Despite her protestations that it didn't matter, she clearly wanted to keep that carrot dangling in front of Louis's nose. Some part of her wanted to keep the idea alive in his mind that if he could only rub her in the right spot in the right way, she would finally reward him with an orgasm.

But it was the martyrdom of Dina's last line—"It just makes me feel good to know that it was good for you"—that conveyed her most telling message: *she had sacrificed for him and now he owed her one.* This was ultimately what it was all about—the trade-off. She had given him sex, now she wanted something in return, and that something was *bigger than sex.*

Almost every couple I know has some element of "you owe me one" in their relationship, particularly in their sexual relationship. She gives him oral-genital stimulation, but he does not return the favor: *he owes her one.* She refused last time he tried to initiate sex: *she owes him one.* She said, "I love you," but he only smiled: *he owes her one.* She came twice, but he only came once: *she owes him one.*

But where was Louis in all this quid pro quo sexuality? *He* was the one who had dragged Dina into my office: *he* was the one who was making an issue out of the fact that she did not have orgasms. Wasn't he just another man trying to "ring his woman's bell" so that he could feel like a stud instead of like a sexual failure? Hadn't he set himself up for a "you owe me one" just by relentlessly asking "Was it good for you, too?" And ultimately, wasn't he the one who was focusing on performance sex to the exclusion of loving feelings?

Certainly there was a large part of Louis's makeup that was pure macho: that's what his list of women whom he had "made come" was all about. But the longer we talked, I sensed another side of Louis coming through, a side that was more frustrated by the loneliness he felt in bed with Dina than by the sense of failure he felt as her lover.

"But what is Dina holding out for?" Louis asked me. "What do you think she wants from me?"

"I think she wants the same thing from you that you really want from her," I told him. "And that's more than just an orgasm. She wants you to give her feelings."

But neither of these compulsive "givers" could feel much until he or she began selfishly taking pleasure for himself.

"You Don't Bring Me Flowers Anymore"

A hospital administrator once mentioned to me that she was having trouble finding a qualified person to run her patient records department.

"It's not easy," she said. "I need somebody smart and conscientious who's a master of detail and has great managerial skills."

"I know where you can find a dozen perfect candidates for the job in one shot," I replied, winking. "Pick anyone from my preorgasmic women's group."

It's the truth. In the late seventies, I started to realize that these groups of women who had never had an orgasm contained a disproportionate number of very bright, highly disciplined superachievers. For example, out of the hundreds I'd worked with, only a handful had gotten less than a B average in high school. Of those who held jobs, an unusually large number had high-paying professional and managerial positions. Those who were homemakers were generally regarded as stunningly proficient and efficient; they kept their homes—and everyone in them —spic and span. Altogether this was a particularly tidy, well-groomed, and neatly coiffed group. In short, these were "good little girls" who had grown up to be "perfect" women.

Indeed, most of the preorgasmic women in my groups readily described themselves as having once been the kind of girls who never got their pinafores dirty, who helped with the chores, took care of younger siblings, did their homework diligently, and never brought home a bad grade. Often the eldest girl in the family, this good girl usually had critical parents who were hard to please; in fact, she was sure that the only way she could ever please them was by denying her own impulses and needs. Not surprisingly, a disproportionate number of these good girls never masturbated. And so the pattern was set: these girls learned *to give up their own pleasure for the sake of parental approval and love.* Now, as grown women in relationships, these good girls were still denying themselves pleasures—and not just sexual pleasure—in hopes of getting love in return. They were still trying their best to please authority except now that authority was the man in their life.

But what happens if the man in her life suddenly decides that what would please him most would be for her to have an orgasm?

Dina fit the profile of a preorgasmic woman to a tee. She was the first born in her family, a model child and student—the good girl *par excellence.* And now, a first-rate executive and model mother and wife, she was the perfect woman. When she came to my office for her initial private session, she wore a neatly tailored tweed suit and did not have one hair out of place.

Once again, Dina's first words to me were that she was perfectly content with her marriage the way it was and the only reason she was here was because Louis had insisted on it. She repeated all this calmly and politely.

"Listen, Dina, why don't we save some time here?" I said, straight-faced. "Why don't you just go home and start faking orgasms—that should keep Louis happy."

"I'm not about to start lying to Louis," Dina replied coolly.

"I'm glad to hear that," I said matter-of-factly. I realized I was not going to get anywhere with Dina unless I pushed hard on her perfect self-control right away. "Then why don't you just go home and *force yourself* to have orgasms?"

Dina stared back at me resentfully.

"I don't think it's that simple," she said.

"For you, Dina? But I thought you were somebody who could do anything you put your mind to."

Dina stared at me a second, then put her hand to her face, and suddenly there were tears trickling down her cheeks. I handed her a tissue.

"That made you angry, didn't it? You've never done anything just for your own pleasure, have you?" I said softly.

Dina was crying because somebody had accused her of being less than perfect. Even worse, I had accused her of that most reprehensible of failings—not being in perfect control of herself. As for so many other good girls, affection and approval had been doled out to Dina only when she performed up to standard and she was terrified of losing that approval if she dropped below standard.

Dina was caught right smack in the middle of an impossible contradiction. To be a good girl meant staying in perfect control and perfect control meant sacrificing her feelings, including her "sloppy" sexual feelings. But to be a perfect wife meant producing an orgasm for her husband. In short, to be good for her husband, she had to stop being so good. She couldn't win for losing.

"You can't have an orgasm for Louis," I told Dina. "It just doesn't work that way. You can only have an orgasm for yourself. And I think it's time you decided you deserved one."

"You make it sound like it's entirely up to me whether I have one or not," Dina said, regaining her composure.

"It *is* up to you," I said. "Maybe you ought to think about what you're afraid you'll lose if you have one."

Dina was caught in a paradox that ran right through her like a fissure. Here she was, the model of self-control, trying to deny that she was in control of her own orgasms. By implying that her husband was in charge of her orgasms—or lack thereof—she could remain perfect; she hadn't failed at this project, *he* had. But at the same time she was saying, in effect, that Louis had the power to give or deny her orgasms. And that, it seems to me, is about as much power as a person can have. Dina felt that she was at Louis's mercy. Feeling like that, of course she had to find a way to get some power back for herself; and so she denied having any interest in orgasms and then proceeded not to have any. (Later she admitted to me that she routinely ran through lists while she was doing sex with Louis: lists of calls to make and tasks to be done—a sure-fire method for guaranteeing sexual numbness.) By holding back her arousal and orgasm, she was holding on to control. Conversely, that meant that if she *did* have an orgasm—and consequently lost all control—she risked losing everything, including, ultimately, Louis's love and approval. She had given Louis so much power that if she didn't control him, he could control her right out of the picture.

On the one hand, Dina was offering the following deal to Louis: "I'll be your perfect wife and geisha—I'll do sex for you any time you ask. And in exchange you'll stay with me, you won't cheat on me, and you'll think I'm perfectly wonderful. But don't ever expect to really 'get' me, because I don't need sex myself."

Yet, on the other hand, Dina was asking for an altogether different deal from her husband: "I give you sex, now make me feel something. Turn me on. Make me feel loved. And above all, make me feel *loving!*"

Like so many grown-up good girls, Dina was starved for feelings. She had spent her entire life so focused on giving that she was virtually incapable of responding. She was an expert at doing—including doing sex—but she was a novice at feeling—including feeling love. And like so many other women, not just good girls, Dina was convinced that it was her man's responsibility to make her feel. "That's the man's job: to turn us on, to make us feel. Right?" It's the same old deal all over again: sex for love, love for sex.

After some prodding, Dina admitted to me that she thought Louis was not fulfilling his end of the deal. In fact, once she started rolling with this idea, Dina realized that she was really very angry at Louis:

"He never goes out of his way to do something nice for me," she told me. "He hardly ever brings home flowers or candy or anything. I even had to remind him to get me a birthday present last year; and the only reason I did that is so it would look right for the kids."

About sex with him, she said, "He was happy for seven years having sex whenever he wanted it, no questions asked. And believe me, it was never very inspiring. Sure, now he's got this orgasm thing on his mind all the time, but if he could get me to have one by pinching my elbow, he'd do it. And I only want an orgasm if it's going to be a loving thing."

Finally, Dina had admitted that at least under one circumstance she wanted an orgasm for herself.

Now we could begin.

A Deal That's Got Nothing for Everybody

Dina and Louis had something in common with most of the couples I see these days: they were both frantically doing sex in hopes of getting loving feelings in return. Louis was working away diligently, desperately seeking that "right move" that would make Dina come so that he could finally stop feeling like he was having sex all alone. He was laboring for that glitter in her eye that would finally show that she really loved him. And Dina was dutifully providing Louis with sex whenever he wanted it—and providing it with perfumes and powders and a pillow under her buttocks—while she waited for him to finally make her experience those loving feelings.

Louis and Dina's marriage was a typical trade-off of the eighties and, typically, it didn't work. Louis was still lonely, longing for intimacy; Dina was still numb, longing for feeling. It was a deal that had nothing for everybody. And there is a simple reason why: *no one can create intimate feelings by simply doing sex.* Ask the Don Juans of the world: the more they do sex (and the more partners they do it with) the lonelier they feel.

The fundamental reason why Dina could not experience an orgasm was because she could not feel *anything:* not anger, not joy, not love. In my preorgasmic women's groups, it frequently turns out that a woman actually has been achieving orgasms all along in some technical physiological sense, but she has missed them—that is, she did not feel them. These are women who are so closed down that they do not feel any sensations, orgasms among them. I told Dina that it would be impossible for her to have her first orgasm together with her husband because at this point she saw it as giving up the only power she had in the relationship. She would have to learn to have her first orgasms by herself and *for herself.* Therapist Lonnie Barbach discovered several years ago that by working with preorgasmic women apart from their partners she had a much higher success rate than Masters and Johnson had working exclusively with partners together. I asked Dina if I could sign her up for one of my preorgasmic women's groups.

"I don't know," she replied, biting on her lip.

"Are you afraid Louis won't approve?"

Dina nodded.

"Well, he asked for it," I said smiling, and for the first time Dina smiled, too.

I've always maintained that one of the reasons we have such a high success rate (over eighty percent) with preorgasmic women is because they are terrific students. They are good girls who do their homework, and in this case the homework is spending an hour alone each day, at first just examining their bodies and genitals and later touching and masturbating themselves. Along the way, we experiment with some assertiveness exercises, another way of getting some feeling back for these perennial self-denying pleasers. But for Dina, as for most of the women in these groups, the final barrier to allowing herself the pleasure of an orgasm was her fear of her husband's disapproval. Yes, Louis *said* he wanted her to have an orgasm, but as a child Dina had learned that she did not get approval or love if she followed her own feelings. Why should this be any different?

Over the years several women who have learned to achieve orgasm in my groups have gone home and pretended to their partners that they were still preorgasmic. They practice the flip side of faking an orgasm; they fake *not* having an orgasm. Both fakers go through their charade for the same reason: to keep their men happy and unthreatened; to keep their men from leaving them.

The unfortunate fact is that there is some truth in these women's fears. Numerous times the very husband who drags his preorgasmic wife into my office to be fixed ends up trying to pull her out of my women's group. He is threatened to the core. "Am I going to be able to satisfy her as well as she can satisfy herself?" he worries. Or worse, "Do I really want a woman who is this sexual? Won't she swallow me up?"

Some husbands are overwhelmed when their wives come home from my group and begin having multiple orgasms. This is more than he bargained for. He becomes afraid that he will not be able to keep up with her, that he is losing some imagined sexual competition, and so he starts criticizing her. He complains that sex has become impersonal for her, that she is too distant. But he never quite says what is really on his mind: he is afraid she is having more fun than he is.

Happily, in Louis's case Dina's fear proved unfounded. To be sure, Louis had initially believed that he alone was responsible for Dina's orgasms just as she had believed. What's more, after only a few weeks in my group, Dina started to become much less organized at home; she let dishes pile up, the housekeeping deteriorate, and began asking Louis to bring home take-out dinners two or three nights a week. She was reveling in her newfound sloppiness and selfishness. But at the same time, she was relating to Louis in an active, loving way for the first time.

"I don't know what came over me," Dina reported to the group one day. "I crept up behind Louis and pinched his behind. For a second there I was scared how he would react, but then he turned around and pinched me back. This may sound funny, but that's the most loving moment I've ever felt with him."

A few weeks later, Dina and Louis were making love together, orgasms and all. They had discovered the only "deal" that really works: they each took pleasure *for themselves* and then shared the feelings that flowed from that pleasure. The Beatles' balance sheet was right: And that, it turns out, is the best deal in town.

 *Chapter 6*

Unfaithfully Yours

I love those ominous magazine articles that list the *Five Top Telltale Signs that Your Husband Is Having an Affair.*

Number 1 is usually some manifestation of his irrepressible guilt, like he cannot look you in the eye anymore, or he is given to sudden bouts of depression, especially at family gatherings. Number 2 alerts you to his new secretiveness ("Does he close the door *before* he answers the phone?") and Number 3 warns you that he may suddenly be paying more attention to his appearance, while Number 4 suggests that you check over his credit card receipts for local hostelries ("Be honest with yourself, is there any plausible business reason why he'd be renting a room at the Old Forge Motel on a Thursday night?")

Number 5, of course, is that dead giveaway: he does not make love to you anywhere near as frequently as he used to and, when he does, he seems guilty and withdrawn.

The people who write those articles must know different couples from the ones I do. (For one thing, I never see articles about the telltale signs that your *wife* is having an affair and yet, judging from my practice, wives seem every bit as active as men in this regard.) In any event, if I were to draw up *my* top five telltale signs based on the couples who have come into my office recently, it would go something like this:

1. He seems freer and more cheerful than usual at home.

2. He keeps dropping clues all over the place to help you detect his infidelity.

3. He is eating better.

4. He leaves his credit card receipts for the Old Forge Motel on top of his dresser (see number 2).

5. He wants to make love to you about twice as often as he used to and, when he does, he seems more relaxed and uninhibited.

I am exaggerating a bit, of course, but the truth is that many of the unfaithful husbands (and wives) I encounter do feel freer and are less sexually inhibited with their spouses than before their extramarital affairs. The reason for this burst of exuberance is that the affair has breathed some air into their claustrophobic marriage; it has created some space in a relationship that had begun to feel like a trap for both of them.

"Hold it right there, Dagmar!" I can hear someone screaming. *"The sixties are over and open marriage was a total catastrophe. You, of all people, aren't going to advocate infidelity as a way of 'freshening up' a marriage, are you?"*

Never. Whatever short-term benefits infidelity can bring to a marriage, its long-term effect is all too often destruction of the marriage. First comes the sense of freedom, but then comes the guilt and recriminations and finally the breakdown of trust. And the sad part is that a couple could breathe that same emotional freedom and sexual exuberance into their marriage without ever going to such a destructive extreme. If they knew how, they could introduce that necessary distance into their relationship without his having to run off with his secretary to the Old Forge Motel.

"Just When We Were Feeling So Close . . ."

"I don't even know what I'm doing here," Kelly Q. announced the moment she sat down in my office. "I can't imagine ever forgiving him for what he's done to me."

"He" was Jack, her husband of ten years who sat next to her with a look of utter desolation and guilt on his large boyish face. Seven months ago, Jack had started sleeping with a floor model at the dress company where he worked, and he had only broken off the relationship the month before when Kelly finally found out about it. The most painful part of it all, Kelly told me, was discovering exactly when Jack's affair had begun.

"We had just spent a weekend at our favorite hotel in the Poconos," she said. "Left the kids at my mother's, danced until the wee hours, breakfast in bed, the whole works. And we made love I don't know how many times, just like in the old days before we got married. It was like falling in love again. For *me*, at least."

Kelly dabbed at her eyes with a handkerchief before going on.

"The very next day—that Monday, I'm telling you—he takes up with his mannequin. I'm home, still dreaming about the Poconos and he's taking a coffee break between her legs. How's that for timing?"

"I didn't plan it that way," Jack protested weakly. "It just happened."

"Like magic, right?" his wife retorted bitterly. "Then who says it's not going to happen again?"

Kelly's message to me was loud and clear: "Punish the S.O.B.! And fix him so he never cheats on me again! Then and only then will I consider forgiving him and getting on with our relationship."

From other betrayed wives this message is communicated with

more subtlety and with greater finesse, but it still comes down to the idea that my job is to retrain their husbands as if they were delinquent boys in need of moral education. Jack, like so many other unfaithful husbands, embraced this role of the "bad boy" almost with relief: as we will see later, being the scoundrel can have its emotional advantages. So Jack was the Sinner and Kelly was the Saint.

I suppose there is a point at which a paradox becomes so common that it ceases to be a paradox. In sex therapy it is almost the *rule* that the person with the "symptom" is, paradoxically, a "front" for the partner with a deeper problem. A wife comes in who is sexually cold and withdrawn and I immediately look for a husband who has sexual insecurities; a husband comes in who is a premature ejaculator and I immediately look for a wife who is sexually anxious and impatient. Similarly, in cases of infidelity, the person with the symptom—the Sinner—is usually acting out a problem that is at least as much his partner's as his own.

But what was the problem that Jack was acting out?

Like Kelly, I was struck by the timing of Jack's infidelity. I asked them both if there was anything unusual about the period immediately prior to their weekend tryst in the Poconos. They both shrugged. No.

"We weren't fighting, if that's what you mean," Kelly said. "We were just living like any other normal couple. More normal than usual, actually, since they took Jack off the road."

It seems that a year earlier Jack had been promoted from traveling salesman to office-based sales manager and ever since he had been home every night for the first time in their marriage. *Home every night after years of being away on the road for weeks at a time!* It sounded like the setup for an unusually difficult period of adjustment to me. I asked them how their physical relationship had gone once Jack was home every night again.

"A little sluggish," Jack answered. "When I was on the road, we always had a big rendezvous thing when I came home. A lot of glad-to-see-you stuff in the bedroom two or three nights in a row. But things kind of got bland after I stopped traveling. Routine, you know?"

But then their lovemaking had picked up again *immediately after* that weekend in the Poconos and the onset of Jack's adulterous affair.

"That's what really makes me burn," Kelly said. "All those months of us going at it every night like born-again lovers and that's the *same* time he's getting it on with his playmate. We were making love with so much feeling and then I find out it wasn't so personal after all. It's humiliating."

"Don't feel humiliated," I assured Kelly. "Jack's affair was his way of going back on the road again—*for both of you.*"

All the pieces fit together now. For the first nine years of Jack and Kelly's marriage, their whole relationship had been predicated on Jack's coming and going, reunions and farewells, periods of being together followed by periods of being alone. It had had a rhythm that worked for both of them, allowing them both to "recover" from bouts of passionate intimacy by pulling back into their individual selves with secure boundaries. But when Jack was suddenly home all the time, something had gone out of their marriage. They had *both* lost some independence, some breathing space, and that had quickly shown up in a lackluster sexual relationship. Even Kelly admitted that they had quickly fallen into a dull bedroom routine, although she failed to take any responsibility for it. And then, when they had their romantic weekend in the Poconos hotel, long afternoons making sensual love, they both experienced a burst of intimate feelings for each other—overwhelming feelings. *But there was no familiar way for either of them to pull back into themselves again.* Jack was not going off on the road afterward: he was driving home together with his wife.

I asked Kelly if she recalled her feelings on the drive home from that romantic weekend and she maintained that she felt loving and happy.

"That's not the way I remember it," Jack interjected. "You got yourself into a rotten mood before we even made it to the turnpike. You kept going on about how all the fun was over and now we were going back to our drab old lives again. You sounded like the kids at the end of summer vacation. You kept whining, 'Why can't we always be like we were back in the hotel? Why can't you be romantic at home too?' It got pretty heavy."

So heavy that Jack found himself in bed with another woman the very next day. Between the overwhelming intimacy of the weekend and Kelly's apparent *demand* for nonstop romance forever after, Jack had run away: straight into another woman's arms. It was his solution to the panic of overwhelming intimacy. For most unfaithful men, one dimension of that panic is his own fear of abandonment; when he is closest to his wife, his fear of losing her grows so great that he flirts with breaking up the marriage himself—at least then he will be in control of his fate. By doing sex with a woman for whom he felt no love, Jack could feel "strong" enough to happily—and intimately—make love with his wife without giving in to his panic.

An affair can also be the solution to the panic of suffocating in intimacy. Untold numbers of husbands suddenly start affairs when their wives are pregnant with their first child—and even more frequently when their wives are pregnant with their second. The trap of family life is closing completely: having sex with another woman is a last desperate declaration of masculine independence. But, of course, it is not a sign of independence at all: it is only a sign of desperate fear.

When I spoke with Jack alone, he assured me that this had been his first and only extramarital affair. This struck even him as odd.

"All those stories about traveling salesmen are true," he said to me. "I know dozens who've got a different woman in every city in their territory. One of the perks of life on the road, right? But I was the exception—Mr. True Blue. Right up until I came home for good."

Jack was beginning to see the connection between "coming home for good"—like a bird with clipped wings—and flying off into another woman's bed.

But what about Kelly? Was she simply the injured party? The martyred saint who had asked for nothing more than love and loyalty from her husband? My guess was that Kelly needed distance in their relationship as much as Jack did—maybe even more. One clue stood out in particular: it was the way Kelly had pestered Jack for "endless love" on that car trip home. That was guaranteed to have the exact opposite effect on him, and at some preconscious level, Kelly knew that. She was using her demand for romance to push Jack away so that she could have some much-needed recovery space of her own. "You'll stop making love to me like that!" she cried in panic. It was a self-fulfilling prophecy that put the blame for any failure in their relationship squarely on Jack's shoulders.

But, of course, Jack had behaved paradoxically too. By embarking on a sexual affair, he could give Kelly the endless love she said that she wanted from him. He became a free and exuberant lover at home. And, because he was also spending more and more time away from home to tend to his affair, he was also giving Kelly the space she needed. It worked right up until Jack could not keep his guilt at bay any longer.

"How could he do this to me just when we were feeling so close?" Kelly asked me.

And my answer was, "He did it precisely *because* you were feeling so close. And neither of you was equipped to handle that much closeness."

How Do You Tell the Good Guys from the Bad Guys?

Jack was finally caught in his infidelity when he left a hotel room key in the pocket of a suit coat that he asked Kelly to bring to the cleaners for him. It was like leaving a fingerprint-covered gun at the scene of the crime. Just as he had "found himself" in bed with another woman, he now "found himself" caught in his indiscretion. Jack managed to convince himself that neither was a conscious act; that way he did not have to assume responsibility for either his crime or his apprehension. When his guilty feelings finally caught up with him, Jack avoided the childlike humiliation of confession by letting Kelly be his accuser and judge. It was her turn to do the acting out. Jack could just be the bad guy.

Given the alternatives, being the Bad Guy is an easy job. The Bad Guy does not have to confront his feelings of weakness or vulnerability—he can just feel guilty. And, if he has had a lot of practice being the Bad Guy, he can even feel sorry for himself as his punisher berates him. Men seem to have a particular aptitude for taking on this role; it is "masculine" to be bad, especially sexually bad. It is still an active role and not a victim's role. A real man can have sex with any number of women, and, when he gets caught, a real man can take his punishment. In fact, he can go through the whole cycle without having to experience very many real feelings at all.

Even so, it is remarkable how many unfaithful men willingly accept the designation of Bad Guy *even when their wives have been unfaithful too.*

"He started it," one wife said to me angrily. "Anything I did later was just a reaction. Just my desperate attempt at getting even, as if I ever could."

This woman's husband did not utter so much as a peep of

protest. Their respective roles of Good Guy and Bad Guy suited them both.

Embracing these roles wholeheartedly is the last and ultimately saddest way of maintaining space in a relationship. In a sense, Jack's job had always been to take care of the distancing in their marriage. First he had very literally provided distance by being on the road much of the time; then he had provided distance by having an affair; and finally he provided distance by being the Bad Guy. He could now stand in the corner while Kelly verbally beat on him—no danger of either of them drowning in intimacy that way.

But neither Kelly nor Jack really wanted to give up on their marriage—that is why they had sought help. I asked them if they were willing to take the first step toward one another by "letting their bodies start to make friends" and they both agreed to try the Graduated Sensual Exercises.

"Just focus on your body's feelings while you're doing the exercises," I told them. "You've got the whole rest of the day to feel angry and guilty."

But, alas, Kelly could not let go of her anger, *especially when it was Jack's turn to tenderly caress her.* She would stop him almost as soon as he began and start yelling and crying all over again.

"All it does is remind me that he did this with *her,*" Kelly said bitterly in my office the following week.

"But I never touched her like that!" Jack retorted. "The only thing I did with her was screw!"

In his way, Jack had just summed up his infidelity perfectly. By doing sex without emotion outside his home, he had been able to continue making love with emotion with his wife. While some men and women avoid the terrors of intimacy by doing sex with their mates, others, like Jack, can avoid those terrors by splitting their lives in half: make love here, do sex there. Kelly, of course, was not appeased by this explanation. The following week, after again trying the first Sensual Exercise, she announced that it simply was not working and she was giving up on therapy altogether.

"Couldn't you focus on your sensual feelings even for a little while?" I asked her.

Kelly shook her head. No.

"Bull!" Jack said. "For a while there, when I was running my hand over your back and legs, you were purring like a kitten."

"Pig!" Kelly cried, her face flushing.

Kelly was humiliated because she had been found out—she really had gotten into her sensual feelings, if only for a little while. But more significantly, she was upset because she thought that letting herself experience those feelings meant that she was "giving in" to Jack, surrendering her pride and her identity. Kelly was, indeed, a sensuous woman who was flooded with strong emotions whenever she made love. That is why afterward she needed so much space to put herself back together again.

"Let's give it one more try," I said. "But this time, immediately after you finish the exercise, I want one of you to leave the house. Really, get out and don't come back for at least two hours."

It worked. I could tell by the smiles on their faces when they walked into my office that next week that it had been a resounding success. By knowing that they would each have some private recovery time afterward, they had been able to make love the way they used to when Jack was still on the road.

"We still sometimes feel the need to do that crazy 'take-a-walk' routine," Kelly told me on the phone recently. "In the dead of winter it can be a real pain, let me tell you. But it beats heck out of the alternative, right? And the best part is that somewhere along the line I started trusting Jack all over again."

"I Hadn't Counted on Falling in Love"

There had never been any question of Jack's being in love with the other woman and this, to some degree, made his infidelity easier to forgive and forget. The distinction between doing sex and making love was fairly clear. But in other cases I see, it gets far more complicated than that.

Miriam L., a dramatic-looking advertising executive, came to see me alone. She was thirty-five years old, married, and had two children. She told me that she loved her husband and children dearly. She also told me that she was madly in love with a man she was having an affair with.

"I know this sounds corny," she told me, "but it wasn't supposed to happen this way. I hadn't counted on falling in love. It never happened before."

In fact, Miriam had had several casual affairs over the course of her twelve-year marriage.

"But they were more like warm bodies than full-fledged affairs," she said. "I felt bad about them, but sex with Greg [her husband] hasn't amounted to much of anything for years, so it was just a way of feeling alive once in a while. Nobody got hurt. I could always keep things separate."

Miriam was describing a kind of arrangement that not long ago had been reserved primarily for husbands: she had uninvolved sex outside the home with virtually anonymous partners; and she had a loving emotional connection (although not much lovemaking) at home with her husband. The perfect split-off deal, as long as she could "keep things separate."

But then she fell in love with one of the "warm bodies."

"It's funny," Miriam told me. "Brad [her lover] is married and the veteran of a lot of affairs, too. That's what made him so 'safe' for me. No demands, no complications. Just enjoy each other and go home. But then, little by little, we started to get into each other in a totally different way."

Miriam told me that she realized her relationship with Brad was changing when they both started to want more time together.

"And it wasn't just for sex either," she said. "Sometimes we just lie together on the hotel room bed, kissing, touching, hugging, talking, listening to music—and then we look at the clock and realize we've got to go home and we never even made love."

It sounded to me like they were making love, just not always feeling the need to move from sensual intimacy to pure sexuality. And I guessed that Miriam was making love (as compared to doing sex) for the first time in a very long while. Indeed, she told me that she had only experienced that kind of lingering sensual intimacy with one other person: with Greg, her husband, during the year they lived together before they got married.

"But that literally stopped the day of our wedding," Miriam told me. "We took our vows and Greg suddenly turned into this passionless prig. At first I thought it was just a phase he was going through, but he never came out of it."

It seemed that Greg, like so many other men and women, had unwittingly reverted to passionless Mom-and-Dad sex the minute he became a family man. Sex with his wife—the future mother of his children and hence a replica of his own mother— could not do the carefree, sensual stuff he had reveled in with his mistress. *Even though wife and mistress were the very same person!*

But why had Miriam so willingly let her husband remain such a "prig" all these years? Was it because it gave her permission to have affairs? And that way she could keep sex and love in separate parts of her life so that she would never have to feel overwhelmed by either?

Before I could get into any of these questions, I had to know what Miriam wanted now.

"I want to disappear," she told me, her eyes brimming with

tears. "I finally have love *and* sex with one person—but he's the *wrong* person!"

I told Miriam that I thought she could combine love and sex with the *right* person, Greg, if she were willing to try. The reason she had gotten into this dilemma in the first place was because she was finally mature enough to be capable of combining the two—and that was the hard part. I said that if both she and Greg were willing to try, they might be able to pick up where they had left off the day they got married. But to attempt that she would first have to end her affair with Brad. I could not work with Miriam and her husband if she were having sexual contact with someone else at the same time. I've tried that and it simply does not work.

"But what if it's too late for Greg and me to start our love life over again?" Miriam asked.

"I can't give you any guarantees," I answered. "Just hope."

Flash forward, as they say in the movies. I did not hear from Miriam again for almost a year, and when I did she told me that she had tried to break up with Brad several times, but kept going back to him.

"It was like trying to give up smoking," she said with a nervous laugh.

But then she had finally realized that if she did not give up Brad, she would have to give up Greg. She knew that she had reached the point in her life where love and sex had to go together and with only one person. She could not keep things separate in her heart any longer. When we spoke, she had not seen Brad for over two months.

"I'm ready to start all over with Greg now," she said, "but I can't bear the idea of telling him about Brad or any of the others. We'd never have a chance then."

I don't hand out moral advice: that's not my business. In some cases, I can sense that a secret will fester and poison a relationship if it is never revealed, but I believed that Miriam could put her past behind her and not let it interfere with her feelings for her husband. And Greg, it turned out, was unusually receptive to therapy and the Sensual Exercises. Literally within weeks, he and Miriam were making tender, sensual love and loving it.

"How did we let so many years go by without doing this?" he asked Miriam in my office.

Tears filled Miriam's eyes.

"I only want to think about all the lovely years ahead of us," she answered.

Jimmy Carter's Lusting Heart

Virtually all the cases of infidelity I hear about are involved, at some level, with the dilemma of how to combine sex and love. A man runs off and has wild sex with a woman he barely knows because he feels inhibited having passionate sex with the woman he tenderly loves—his wife. A sensual woman chooses a sexually reluctant man for her husband and then finds herself having one affair after another with men she can make no emotional connection with. These people cannot deal with love and sex in the same place, so they end up commuting between them.

Lately, I've been seeing a new variation on this dichotomy: what I call the Sexless Extramarital Affair. Once again, sex and love are separated, but this time uninvolved sex remains at home with the spouse and passionate-yet-unconsummated love is with someone else—usually someone at the work.

Aaron S., a forty-five-year-old physician, typifies this syndrome. He has been married for fifteen years to an attractive Scandinavian nurse he met when he was in medical school, but he is almost always carrying on a chaste but terribly romantic affair with another woman, usually a doctor at his hospital. At home, he does sex regularly with his wife; at the hospital, he has romantic lunches where he gazes into his current beloved's eyes and curses the unfairness of life which keeps them apart.

Aaron's setup seems harmless enough, there's no reason why anyone should get hurt. Indeed, such chaste affairs could be a legitimate way of injecting some space into one's relationship at home. But by always yearning for some other woman, Aaron was avoiding loving feelings at home. His everyday feelings for his wife could not begin to compete with the heightened romantic feelings he had in his unconsummated relationships. Like real philanderers, he had managed to keep love and sex separate so as not to be threatened by either, but frustrated by both.

"I think you need to learn how to be more 'promiscuous,' not less," I told Aaron. "While you're being 'unfaithful' to your wife, why don't you carry on these romantic flirtations with two or three women at once?"

For an experiment, I asked him to have lunch in the hospital cafeteria with a different attractive woman each day of the week and to fall in love with as many as he could.

Two weeks later Aaron returned to my office with a silly grin on his face. He had, indeed, been smitten by a second and then a third beautiful intern at the hospital, but in the process, something else had happened too: he had begun to make love with more feeling with his wife.

"I give up," he said to me. "What's going on?"

"You've found out that your feelings aren't as exclusive as you thought," I told him. "In fact, you can fall in love with your wife, too, along with the rest."

But more important, having three romantic flirtations going on at once gave Aaron the space he needed to feel less threatened by combining love and sex at home.

Other than presidential candidates and deeply religious people, most folks are not troubled by occasionally lusting in their hearts for someone other than their mates. It only becomes a problem I hear about when they find that they are almost *always* fantasizing about someone else when they are having sex with their spouse. Or, more distressingly, when they find that they can only *feel sexually aroused* with their husband or wife if they close their eyes tightly and imagine they are making love with someone else: a movie star, next-door neighbor, or lover from years ago. Like infidelity, these fantasies provide the distance some people need to let go with their sexual feelings. By fantasizing that they are in bed with someone else, they imbue the whole bedroom scene with an air of unreality. It is like a sexual dream, uncluttered by the everydayness and the petty angers that inevitably accumulate between husband and wife.

Again, there is no harm done, is there?

Only when it begins to feel as if it is cheapening the experience, when it feels like another way to do sex instead of making love.

"Here I've been making love to Robert Redford," one woman told me. "And then I open my eyes, kiss Harold, and tell him I love him. It feels a little hollow to say the least."

Most people have sexual fantasies several times a day. They can be set off by a wisp of odor, a glimpse of thigh, the brush of an elbow, an idle memory of a long-ago lover. I am all for fantasies. They keep us sexually alert and alive; they keep open cracks in our armor against everyday sensuality. But when fantasy becomes a *total substitute* for real intimacy, we inevitably start coming up against those old complaints: "I feel numb" and "I feel lonely after we have sex" and "I've lost that loving feeling."

It would be a mistake to abruptly drop all fantasies, keep our eyes wide open, and bring "Harold" thudding back in our love life all at once. The end effect would be only to kill all our feelings, sexual and romantic. Like an overloaded electrical system, we would short out.

"Don't get rid of your fantasies," I tell people. "But start giving your mate a 'walk-on' once in a while."

While you are lying alone in the warm bathtub gently caressing your belly and breasts, imagine for a moment that it is your husband who is caressing you. Redford had his turn, let Harold have his. Little by little, you can let an "imaginary" Harold into your fantasy life and next time you are lying in bed with your eyes tightly closed as the *real* Harold caresses you, you can start to merge these two Harolds. It is a funny bit of mental gymnastics, but it can ease the way to that ultimate merger of love and sex that is known as making love.

 *Chapter 7*

Safe Sex:
The Silver Lining

Let there be no mistake about it: the AIDS epidemic affects us all, straight as well as gay, female as well as male, married as well as single. This tragedy and the terror that accompanies it has altered the very meaning of sexuality.

In the hospital where I work, I have seen the ravaged victims of AIDS and it is unbearably sad. Others have written movingly and eloquently about their agony; I will not presume to add to that literature of suffering. Nor is it my intention here to offer to the worried well technical instruction. There are safe sex manuals and kits available to everyone who has the good sense to want to enjoy sex with a minimum of risk. No, my purpose is to explore how the specter of AIDS shapes our thoughts and feelings about *all* sex: how it confirms irrational fears as well as real fears; how it can be used as an excuse in the service of other anxieties for avoiding sex altogether; how it affects our attitude toward monogamy and infidelity; and how it even intrudes on our sexual fantasies. But I also want to show how AIDS and other sexually transmitted diseases, such as herpes, have created a new climate of candor between the sexes and how, ultimately, it can help us become connoisseurs of intimate, sensual lovemaking.

The "Touch Kills" Conspiracy

In moments of unbridled paranoia, I am sure there is a conspiracy going on out there to undo whatever good we sex therapists have accomplished over the years. I had just convinced my women's groups that the vagina was a strong and healthy organ when —zap!—along came toxic shock syndrome. And I was just beginning to convince couples that there was nothing unhealthy about tasting semen when semen was found to be a potential medium for transmitting the AIDS virus. Half of my work as a sex therapist is to free people from the inhibiting belief that sex is dirty and dangerous—and now we are warned constantly that it is both.

There is no conspiracy, of course; these are not manmade plagues. And the dangers of sexually transmitted diseases are very real. But it is also true that individuals and institutions are using the current AIDS scare to advance their own cause of chastity and sexual isolation. Sexual inhibition is becoming legitimized, sexual phobia the norm.

In the movie *David and Lisa*, the film classic about two young people who fall in love in a mental institution, David is terrified of any physical contact. "Touch kills!" he cries, wincing in horror as he recoils from even the most lovingly offered hand. He is the pathetic embodiment of every hysterical mother's warning: "Don't put that in your mouth! There are germs everywhere!" and "Wash your hands! You don't know who touched that!" David retreated into a world of total isolation, into a self-made antiseptic dome where he was perfectly safe. And where he was unbearably lonely.

I am worried that the AIDS scare will make us into a "Touch kills!" society. I see it beginning to happen already.

In the psychiatric wards of my hospital, we are seeing a growing number of psychotics with exaggerated AIDS phobias: a woman who wears a surgical mask in the subway because she is sure she can get AIDS from an errant sneeze; a man who blows a police whistle and shouts "Black death!" whenever he sees an obvious homosexual in the street. As always, a wave of psychotic extremes tells us the fears that lurk at the center of society. Lately, a disturbing number of "well-adjusted" people have told me it is a "fact" that one can get AIDS from a toilet seat. Just when we were recovering from the myth that we could get pregnant from toilet seats! And recently I have been to several parties where intelligent, supposedly well-informed people reflexively back away from their gay friends and dodge greeting them with a kiss on the cheek.

But when we give in to *every* unfounded fear in the name of "better safe than sorry," we run the risk of totally isolating ourselves. Not just sex stops, but all sensual contact with one another stops. Even kissing and touching become suspect. The enemies of sensuality finally win their battle. In chorus, the President, the Church, and Mom sing out triumphantly: "That's right, abstain from everything! *Touch kills!*"

Their song echoes daily in my office. At my hospital I run an Over Thirty Virgins group, mostly professional women who yearn to overcome their formidable inhibitions and finally enjoy their first sexual experience. For years, it was one of my most popular groups with a surprising number of virgins streaming in for help. But recently their number dropped radically and I wondered why.

"It's an advantage to be a virgin these days, not a handicap," one group member informed me. "I know a lot of virgins who are running personal ads in the papers declaring their untouched status. That's what men are looking for these days, so if you've got it, flaunt it."

I am certainly happy that some people are benefiting from the current hysteria, but I do wonder how they will fare once their ads work. When sexual fears and inhibitions are prerequisites for an acceptable mate, we can expect a great number of sexually unsatisfying marriages. Guaranteed safe partners often turn out to be guaranteed sorry lovers.

Most distressingly, I am seeing an increasing number of single men and women who hide behind sexually transmitted diseases as a way of evading confrontation with their personal sexual problems. A recent *New Yorker* cartoon pictured a rigid-looking man sitting alone on a couch in a three-piece suit watching television; the caption was "Safe Sex." AIDS is a godsend for the sexually troubled, the catchall excuse for giving up on all contact with the opposite sex. One young man I worked with suffered from periodic bouts of impotency. Since his last humiliating episode, he had completely stopped dating women. In therapy, he and I began gradually probing a personal history of fear of women which dated back to his early childhood. It was a painful process, but he was just getting to the root of his problem when he suddenly announced to me with undisguised relief that even if he got his potency back, "with AIDS around, I'd be crazy to do anything with it." These were not the words of a man who was actively seeking recovery.

In another instance, a thirty-five-year-old woman with a long-standing phobia of kissing brought me a different article every week that "proved" that AIDS could be spread via saliva. Like so many people, she would rather believe hysterical rumors than deal with her own sexual anxieties. "See! I'm right!" these clients say to me triumphantly. "I'm not sick, I'm prudent." But then, of course, they go home, still sexually troubled and isolated—and AIDS has nothing to do with that.

Not only does the indeed very serious AIDS scare play into

our sexual fears and phobias, it also feeds our neurotic distrust of one another. In particular, it abets the war between the sexes. Men can again be seen as selfish soilers, women as dangerous Jezebels. Every hysterical warning Mother gave us is confirmed: "Men don't care what happens to you, as long as they get their way"; "You never know where he's put that 'thing' before he put it in you"; and "She's sexy, all right, but that's just the kind of girl you could pick up something awful from."

When normal heterosexual contact can transmit a fatal disease, men and women are natural enemies.

"You Bring the Wine, I'll Bring the Condoms"

But there really is a silver lining to all this. Our preoccupation with safe sex has forced many of us to become much more candid with each other than was ever possible before. And as a result, many of us who might have been too guilty, panicked, or shy to even mention sex are now open, patient, and, when need be, even assertive about sex. Too much is at stake now for us to have any dirty little secrets anymore and what a relief it is to have them out in the open.

Restaurants buzz with sex talk these days. Over Oysters Casino, one young woman tells her date that she's had three consecutive lovers over the past four years and one, in particular, worried her so much that she went and got the AIDS test. It was negative, how about you? At the next table over spaghetti carbonara, a young man is saying to his date that he hasn't gone to bed with anyone in six months because he just can't be casual about sex anymore. He's only interested in a steady sexual relationship now, how about you? And at the table behind them, a rather demure-looking woman is telling her date that she never thought she'd ever get used to condoms, but now she kind of likes them, especially the new, multicolored ones, how about you?

"First dates these days are the longest in history," one single woman told me. "True confessions from start to finish—it's better than group therapy. And by the time you kiss each other good night, you know all of each other's vital statistics: who they've slept with, when's the last time they were tested, what they like to do in bed. Only after all that's out of the way do you talk about what your favorite movies are."

Most single people I've spoken with find this new sexual *glasnost* quite liberating. It is not just that their concerns about safe sex are answered, but *all* sexual tension is broken between them. Sexual guilts are quickly relieved, sexual predilections are painlessly discussed.

"It used to be that whenever I got into a relationship I'd immediately start dreading that moment when I would have to tell about this sordid affair I had years ago with a married man," one woman told me. "It's not exactly something I'm proud of. But now it comes out first thing, my anxiety's gone, and we can get on to the more important business of seeing how we feel about each other."

And a single, middle-aged man told me that it used to be difficult for him to even bring up the subject of oral sex with a woman, let alone initiate it with her, and as a result he usually ended up denying himself this form of sexual gratification.

"Now it's all part of the same conversation," he told me. "I say something like, 'Well, I hear cunnilingus is still supposed to be safe, which is terrific because it happens to be one of my favorite things,' and there it is, right out there on the table."

There is sort of a trickle-down effect to this general openness that makes all sexual subjects easier to talk about, even in that most tongue-tying of places, the bedroom.

"I could never tell a lover that I happened to like a particular position," a thirty-five-year-old woman told me. "Now, after discussing who's going to bring the wine and who's going to bring the condoms, it's easier to say, 'By the way, I like to be on top once in a while.' "

Yet there are still many people—most often men—for whom this safe sex candor can be off-putting.

"I met this very attractive woman at a wedding reception," a man in his early forties told me. "We danced a few times, getting closer and closer, and then she pulled my head down and whispered in my ear, 'I think you ought to know that condoms are nonnegotiable.' That's love talk in the eighties for you."

We have to develop a new sexual etiquette for the Age of Safe Sex. Openness does not have to mean bluntness; candor does not necessarily have to be unromantic. Instead of saying "Condoms are nonnegotiable," it might be more effective to say, "I was hoping I'd meet somebody like you tonight—that's why I came prepared."

Requesting a new lover to get the AIDS test can also be a tricky business. My gay patients, who have had to confront the specter of AIDS for many years, now take such a request for granted, but most heterosexuals are still fumbling for a way of making this request that will not push a prospective partner away. An AIDS test may be nonnegotiable, but it can still be presented in a positive way, such as, "Wouldn't it be wonderful if we could make love without having to worry? Why don't we both get the test?" It would make us feel a little safer.

For many couples, taking the AIDS test together is tantamount to taking a pledge of fidelity to each other.

"It's the new way of going steady," one humorous young woman told me. "It's like Betty Lou comes rushing into the locker room all a-twitter and says, 'Billy just asked me to get the AIDS test with him. I thought he'd never ask.' "

Yet, like any form of commitment, there are those who will

feel rushed by a request for an AIDS test. But once again, there is value in putting our cards on the table.

"I've been having a kind of casual affair with this guy," a thirty-ish divorcée told me. "And now he wants me to get the test with him. I'm not sure I'm ready for anything that serious."

"You can take the AIDS test without promising a thing," I told her. "You don't have to wear his high school ring if you don't want to."

But as has always been true in matters of sex, there sometimes comes a point where etiquette stops and self-respect and assertiveness have to begin. I frequently hear stories of men who get resentful or worse when a woman pulls a condom out of her purse or bed table drawer. For some men, this act of enlightened self-interest is too "aggressive" and "unfeminine." In other words, they feel threatened, even emasculated by it. I have the same reaction now as I did long before sexually transmitted diseases loomed so large in our consciousness: *Don't let him talk you out of what you know you want. You always feel better when you take charge of your own sex life.*

By the same token, don't allow anyone to badger you into believing that precaution spells the end of romance. I have little patience with those men and women who argue that if you have to rush off to get an AIDS test before you can go to bed, all the romance goes out of sex. I heard the same argument against contraception long ago—that if you stop to put in a diaphragm, you lose "the mood." Nonsense. Just as you can make the insertion of a diaphragm into a playful, sexy game, so can the rolling on of a condom become a part of sex play rather than an interruption of it. Women, roll it on your partner slowly and sensually, caressing your partner's penis and testicles as the condom goes on. And you need not be somber about this act either.

"It seemed so antiseptic at first," one man told me, "like I was being fitted with some surgical device. But then my partner started talking to my penis, telling 'him' how nice he looked in his new English trench coat and we both cracked up."

What getting AIDS tests, inserting diaphragms, and rolling on condoms all have in common is that they make you responsible for what you are doing. And being responsible for your sex life is the first step to making love.

Which brings me to the main reason why I think singles sex in the AIDS era has the potential for creating a whole generation of sensuous love makers. Ironically, the specter of sexually transmitted diseases gets men and women to do what I've always urged them to do—*to slow down their sex lives.* Caution has forced potential lovers to focus on the feelings and attractions that precede genital contact; to linger with these feelings and let them develop gradually and *consciously;* and to bring the total body into lovemaking as they luxuriate in all the sensations awakened by kissing and caressing one another all over.

"I was a veteran bed hopper until this scare hit," one single man told me. "And I hate to admit it, but I had no idea what I was missing. Like all this talking about sex before you ever get near it is a real turn-on. And petting—I always thought that was something that only existed in fifties beach movies, but now everybody's petting again. It's like we've rediscovered this marvelous lost art."

And a divorcée I know said, "I guess throughout all that casual sex, I was looking for a way to know if there's any real feelings involved. Now, I'm allowed to find out first."

Ultimately, caution has forced us to return to old-fashioned sex where you know and trust and care about one another *before* you go to bed.

"Aha! Just as I thought, Dagmar, you're as conservative as the chastity belt types you were complaining about," I hear someone protesting. *"Next you're going to tell us that we really ought to wait until we're married to 'do it.'"*

Wrong. What I'm pleased about is that new couples are not *just* 'doing it,' they are also getting back to all the intimate feelings that precede 'doing it.' They are discovering that touch does not kill; rather it creates love, security, and vitality. I am only sad that it has taken a tragedy to awaken so many of us to this understanding.

"I Can't Even Have a Good Extramarital Fantasy Anymore!"

Let's face it, monogamy never had more to recommend it. In the Age of AIDS, it is definitely the safest way to go. Yet the threat of AIDS even hovers over the marital bedroom, influencing thoughts, feelings, and behavior. Some marrieds revel in the safe haven that marriage affords them while others find that the very idea of *needing* a safe haven makes marriage feel more claustrophobic than ever. This new pressure to make marriage work—because the alternative is so fraught with danger—does not feel very "sexy" at all to some people.

"All my married friends are so self-satisfied," one husband told me recently. "They go on and on about what a horrible time it is to be single and 'Thank God we're married.' But I find being married in these times is a pretty desperate business too. It's like the best thing anybody can say about it is that it's a low-risk venture. Even fidelity isn't a symbol of love and loyalty anymore, it's just an act of self-preservation. Pretty romantic, huh?"

Indeed, AIDS has redefined the very meaning of fidelity—and infidelity. The idea that having an extramarital affair can put your spouse at a serious health risk transcends all other considerations. It is no longer merely a question of loyalty and ego, it is a question of personal survival. In particular, married men who once were able to rationalize their dalliances with prostitutes as harmless have to face the potential awful consequences of their behavior. In my office, the question of sexually transmitted diseases almost always comes up in cases of infidelity. The cry, "How could you do that to me?" is the cry of someone who sees the shadow of murder in the betrayal. Before any bridges can be mended—if that is still a possibility—an AIDS test has to be taken.

On the other hand, several married people have admitted to me that now that adultery is no longer an option, they are relieved.

"It's like at last I have a good excuse for not giving in to my compulsive Don Juan-ism," a husband told me.

But the absence of alternatives—even *imagined* alternatives—can take its toll, too. A forty-year-old married woman I know said to me, "I had no trouble being a contented, faithful wife when the fantasy of making it with a tall, dark stranger was still alive, but these days I can't even have a decent extramarital *daydream* without alarms going off in my head. I don't know about you, but I can't get off on a fantasy about Russian roulette. So somehow I end up resenting the idea that my husband is the only game in town. 'Safe' just feels boring."

At the other end of the spectrum, but with the same result, one married man I worked with admitted, "I used to envy all my single and divorced friends. It seemed like they were having twice as much sexual fun as I was. Now I know they aren't and instead of envying them, I pity them."

This was a man whose wife had complained that he had lost interest in sex lately. Apparently his old sexual motivation of competing with his single friends no longer worked for him. AIDS, in a convoluted way, had become his excuse for avoiding intimate contact with his wife.

And he is not alone in feeling the dampening effects of the AIDS tragedy on his marital sex life. Other married people have said to me that the world just does not feel as sexy as it did before sex became so ineluctably connected to sickness and death.

"Sex, even with the one person you know is safe, will never feel as carefree as it once did," one wife told me. "The Sexual Revolution is now officially over, and we lost."

But if sex does not feel as carefree, it does feel much more intimate to many of the married people I have spoken to. They tell me that the fact that their spouse is "the only game in town" makes them more appreciative, not less. Their awareness of the dire alternatives to monogamy has forced them to focus more intently on one another and that stirs deep feelings in them.

"I feel there's something so much more personal about our sex life these days," one husband told me. "It's like we're making tender love in the eye of this raging storm."

And one wife put it in these stark yet moving terms: "Now, when we offer our bodies to each other, we are literally entrusting each other with our lives. Fidelity has never meant more. Making love is an act of faith. No wonder I feel so much."

 *Chapter 8*

Merging Love
and Sex

The story of Lydia and Marc L. is a sad story with a happy ending. It is about two people who once loved each other deeply, but who virtually destroyed that love because neither of them was capable of combining loving feelings with sexual feelings. By the time they reached my office at the end of their second year of marriage their capacity for emotional intimacy was dying fast and their physical relationship had degenerated to routine and dispassionate genital contact. They were doing sex, but they had long ago ceased making love.

"He doesn't look at me, he doesn't kiss me, he doesn't even say anything to me—it's like having sex with a stranger," Lydia complained during their initial meeting with me. "Except it's lonelier, because I can still remember what a wonderful lover Marc once was."

"And I can still remember when you had soul!" Marc shot back bitterly.

This pair agreed on only one thing: that they had once been madly in love. Both successful cardiologists, Marc was thirty-two and Lydia twenty-nine when they met at a medical congress in New Orleans where Marc was delivering a paper on laser angioplasty.

"My heart literally skipped a beat when I looked at him up there on the podium," Lydia told me. "I felt like some weak-kneed damsel in a paperback romance. All I was thinking was, 'Who is this gorgeous hunk who is talking circles around all these dull doctors—and can I have him, *please?*' "

Marc, too, clearly remembered his instant attraction to Lydia when he met her at a reception after his talk.

"She glowed," he told me. "Not just a beauty thing. She glowed with intelligence and warmth and humor and womanliness. It actually occurred to me right then and there to ask her to marry me."

Their affair started that evening in the New Orleans hotel. For Lydia, that night of lovemaking was unlike anything she had ever experienced before.

"I was relatively inexperienced for a woman my age," she said. "I'd been so involved with school and career that sex had been pretty infrequent and never very satisfying up to then. But I came alive that night. Marc made love to me until the sun rose and I think I had more orgasms in those ten hours than I'd had in my entire life before."

Five months later they were married and almost immediately Lydia started complaining that Marc wasn't as attentive a lover as he used to be.

"She's forever harkening back to that holy night we met and why can't it be like that every night?" Marc said. "She's relentless. No wonder I got turned off to her. I feel like I'm in competition with this ghost of myself in New Orleans."

"But you *did* change! Overnight!" Lydia cried out. "You turned into a sexual automaton the minute we got married!"

At this point, I could see that this bright, articulate couple expected me to referee their ongoing debate over which came first, Lydia's constant demands for lovemaking "the way it used to be" or Marc's withdrawn, coldhearted sex. Like so many stalemated couples, their relationship had been reduced to a childlike fight of "You started it!"—"No, *you* started it!" But to me that was like debating which came first, the chicken or the egg, and just about as productive. What Marc and Lydia had to accept was that *both of them* were having serious trouble merging their loving feelings with their sexual feelings.

It is one of the great tragedies of modern life that love and sex seem so incompatible. Here we are in a culture that prizes lifelong monogamy, that sends us searching for a mate to love, cherish, and have sex with for the rest of our lives, and when we finally find that mate we discover that it was easier to have sex with someone we don't love so much. Something, it seems, must be seriously wrong with the whole system.

"Maybe the old Mormons knew something we don't," one unhappily married man told me. "If I had three or four wives, I'd feel less suffocated and more alive with each. Hell, I'd probably be a better husband and lover to each one of them than I am to my one wife now. Why fight it?"

Why, indeed?

Yet the fact is, culture-bound or not, almost every man and woman I know longs to love *and* make love with the same person. They, like Marc and Lydia, long to know the secret of merging love and sex in one relationship.

"I Love You, Get Lost!"

When I met privately with Marc a few days later, I asked him how he dealt with not feeling turned on by his wife anymore and he told me that he had to resort to playing mental games on himself in order to "get it up." Marc's basic mental game was closing his eyes and pretending that Lydia was someone else. Most people occasionally zip up their sex lives by having a sexual fantasy about someone other than the partner lying there expectantly beside them in bed.

"It offers the thrill of variety without the mess of infidelity," as one woman friend of mine elegantly put it.

I certainly find nothing wrong with that. For many people, occasionally superimposing an imaginary lover onto their regular mate can be the first step in breaking out of a tired sexual routine; with "someone new" they find it easier to try "something new"—say, a new position or even a sexual variation that they have felt too inhibited to try before. It can bring the whole dimension of fantasy back into a bedroom that has been bound by too much serious literalness. There are some couples who can even share their fantasies, making it into an open game that they both participate in.

"About once a month, we do a love scene from one of our favorite movies, complete with props—anything from *Gone With the Wind* to *A Man and a Woman,*" one wife told me. "If we aren't laughing too hard, we have fabulous sex, and if we are laughing too hard, who cares?"

Again, she found no objection from me. In fact, when a fantasy is shared in this way, there is less risk of totally "erasing" the real person with whom you are playing the game. But what about when a fantasy lover completely and consistently replaces your bedmate, when the fantasy lover becomes a necessary condition for feeling sexual at all, as it had for Marc?

I asked Marc if any particular woman "starred" in his fantasies and he said no, that it was someone different almost every time, just as he had slept with someone different almost every time when he was still single.

"The joke's on me, right?" he said unhappily. "One reason I was so ecstatic when I met Lydia was because I could finally be finished with that empty life of rotating bed partners. I thought I'd grown up at last. I'd finally connect with a woman in all kinds of ways, not just sexually. But now I'm back to where I started, only worse."

For Marc, fantasy was not making him feel any sexier, only lonelier. It was not enlivening his sexual relationship with Lydia; on the contrary, it was reducing it to mechanical, unfeeling sex.

It would be easy to simply think of Marc as a Don Juan who was trapped in the pattern of flitting from woman to woman, losing interest as soon as he had made a conquest. Then we could say that he was stuck with sexual feelings that only responded to a challenge—and a wife, after all, is rarely a challenge. In fact, once married, she can easily become perceived as the very opposite, an obligation.

But I wasn't satisfied that the Don Juan theory adequately described Marc's makeup. It turned out that although he had changed sexual partners from one night to the next when he was single, most of the women he slept with were "repeats"—women he had ongoing but casual sexual relationships with. In general, he told me, the women he'd been with were "modern ladies who weren't into coy games; they wanted to get down to business as quickly as I did." He denied experiencing these women as "conquests" and I believed him.

Likewise, it would be tempting to think of Marc as having a Madonna/Whore complex, a man who divided the world of women into either impersonal sex objects, impure and erotic, or personal love figures, pure and untouchable, the former for sex and the latter for setting upon a pedestal and marrying. Typically, men with this complex can only perform sexually with "inferior" women and they can only marry "proper" women, a dichotomy that usually leads to sexless marriages.

But again, Marc did not fit neatly into this category either. For one, the women he had been sleeping with prior to marriage were hardly his inferiors; most, in fact, were educated professionals like Lydia. Nor would it be accurate to say that Marc had a sexless marriage; he dutifully continued to do sex with his bride on a regular basis; he just did not do it with any passion or feelings of intimacy.

And intimate feelings, I suspected, were what Marc feared the most. The Lydia he fell in love with was not a "Madonna"; she was something even more threatening to him: *a real person with whom he felt connected "in all kinds of ways, not just sexually."* He recognized his attraction to Lydia as mature, a step up from the limited affairs he'd had before. Up to that point, he had been satisfied sexually with his various bed partners, but dissatisfied emotionally—isolated, unconnected. But what kept him from being able to enjoy sexual *and* emotional satisfaction with the same person? Why couldn't he love Lydia body *and* soul?

I asked Marc if his languorous, all-night lovemaking with Lydia early in their affair had ever made him feel anxious.

"God, yes, starting with our first night together," he said, looking at me as if I had just read his mind. "We made love, we laughed, we told our life stories, and then we made love again, laughed again, even shed a few funny little tears. I had never felt so close to another human being in my life. It was wonderful, all those feelings coursing through my veins. But then, yes, I started to feel kind of itchy and then that itchiness started to feel like panic. I didn't want to admit it to myself—and I certainly didn't want Lydia to know—but I couldn't wait for her to leave. I was madly in love already, but I wanted her to get lost fast so I could be alone for a little while."

"And put yourself back together again?" I asked.

"Exactly," Marc replied, sounding relieved that I'd understood him.

For all Marc's sexual experience, it is safe to say that the first time he ever "made love" was with Lydia and that experience touched off new and powerful feelings in him, feelings of intimacy and feelings of emotional vulnerability. Marc accurately described his responses to this burst of new emotions as "panic." Here he was finally in a "grown-up" relationship and what was he doing? Laughing and shedding "funny little tears" very much like a child. He felt like he was losing control of himself, and, for a man especially, that can feel very, very dangerous. Once Marc was married, there was no escaping that danger, especially with a wife who constantly demanded intimacy. So Marc reflexively retreated into his tried and true method for staying in control of his emotions: he went back to doing sex.

But just doing sex with Lydia was no easy matter either. She was still the woman who had elicited all those powerful feelings from him; she was still, in fact, the woman he loved. The only way he could "get it up" now was by suppressing all his emotions and pretending that Lydia was someone else, someone to whom he had no real connection. *Marc did not feel safe combining love and sex, so he opted for sex without feeling.*

Given the option between love and sex, most men are sure they can live without love, but not without sex—*even if the sex they've been having is consistently unsatisfying.* It is not, it seems, the sexual experience itself that they need, but the *idea* of it. A man thinks he is not a man unless he does "it" some specific number of times per week or month. Untold numbers of men have come into my office seeking remedies for their dull or nonexistent sex lives, declaring that they feel abnormal—abnormal, not frustrated. But seldom has a man come into my office and told me that he would feel abnormal if he did not have a hug or a tender moment with his wife at least once a week. And I do not think this is because he "needs" the hug less.

Still, it was not only Lydia who was unhappy with what had become of her and Marc's relationship. Marc was miserable, too. He felt more isolated and lonely than when he never experienced real intimacy.

"I'm turning into the Tin Man," Marc told me. "No heart. The sex just makes me feel more estranged from Lydia each time."

In focusing on Marc's fear of intimacy, it is easy to forget that he also *craved intimacy.* That need is what drew him to Lydia in the first place. Much has been written about men's fear of commitment and their inability to sustain intimacy; producing books about husbands who always have their mouths closed, their ears shut, and one foot out the door has become a major industry. But it only tells half the story. We have too readily accepted the simplistic model that portrays women as the ones starving for intimacy and men as the ones who are withholding it. That is not all there is to it. Recent studies demonstrate that most men crave intimacy every bit as much as women do and that the loneliness they feel when deprived of it is equally as devastating. The major difference, it seems, is that men have greater difficulty admitting to and expressing their need for intimacy than women do.

Marc, then, was torn between his fear of intimacy and his need for it. Yes, his fear had led him to retreat to the detached sex of his bachelor days. He was suppressing his emotions to keep his genitals performing. But that is not where it ended, because once Marc was back feeling "unconnected," he started longing for intimacy all over again. Until he could merge love and sex, he was doomed to feeling unfulfilled.

Pushing for Intimacy

But Marc, I suspected, was not alone in his ambivalence toward intimacy. Although Lydia constantly complained about Marc's "eyes closed, mouth shut, hands-on-the-mattress" sex, I was pretty sure that at least one part of her was encouraging her husband to remain a coldhearted lover.

What struck me immediately about Lydia was the provocative way she presented herself. She wore a low-cut blouse and a short, tight skirt which, combined with her rather theatrical makeup, gave her a bigger-than-life appearance. This hardly jibed with the image of a woman who had been so preoccupied with school and career that, until recently, sex had been relatively unimportant to her. When I saw Lydia alone, I asked her if she had always dressed so sexily.

"No," she said with a little shrug of annoyance. "But then again, I'm not as uptight as I used to be."

My guess was that Lydia's appearance was hardly the result of newfound sexual confidence. I should admit right here that whenever I see a woman who presents herself in a particularly provocative manner, I immediately suspect that not only is she overcompensating for a lack of sexual confidence, but for a lack of sexual feeling. Her pose often turns out to be a challenge that says, "Are you man enough to satisfy a woman like me?" And the answer, of course, is that *no* man can make her feel anything because she won't let him. Lydia's appearance struck me as saying, *"Look at me! It certainly can't be my fault that my husband's not turned on by me!"*

"Do you think it's your responsibility to keep Marc perpetually turned on?" I asked her.

Lydia's face abruptly collapsed in a look of soft sadness.

"If it is," she said, "I don't seem to be doing a very good job of it, do I?"

"But it's an *impossible* job," I told her. "He has to turn himself on—and so do you!"

And that, in a nutshell, is the most fundamental message I try to get across to couples. It also seems to be the hardest for them to believe. Because the paradoxical corollary of this message is that only after you forget about your partner and start focusing on your own feelings can you begin to put love and sex back together again. Selfishness is the prerequisite for sexual and emotional intimacy. That may go against all the "ethics" we've ever learned, all the precepts that say that loving is pure selflessness, but it is the dynamic truth in a relationship. *Because until you feel, you have nothing to share.*

It takes a huge leap for most women and men to accept this

and Lydia was no exception. Clearly, Lydia was terrified that she would lose Marc if she could not keep him turned on. From the start, she had felt sexually enthralled by him; she maintained that she "came alive" sexually that first night when *he* made love to her. *He* had given her the orgasms that she'd missed all those years. *He* was the man with sexual experience while she was the novice. In her mind, sex was what had created their relationship and sex could destroy it. She was convinced that she needed Marc to feel sexual and that she needed to be sexy to keep him. The slightest indication that Marc's ardor was dimming sent Lydia into a panic of insecurity and that panic prompted her to act more and more sexually provocative. But ironically, and sadly, all this did was push Marc even farther away from her.

I recalled Marc's rude cry: "I remember when you had soul!" Was this merely the lament of an insecure man who needed his wife to be innocent, demure, and sexually reticent so that he could feel macho and in control? I think not. I believe Marc missed Lydia's genuine warmth, vulnerability, and easy enthusiasm, all those qualities that had allowed *him* to feel so alive at the beginning of their affair. But Lydia was so focused on her sexual insecurity that she could not see that these were the qualities that her husband had fallen in love with. Marc needed little encouragement to retreat from intimacy into his habitual impersonal sex, and Lydia was giving him all the encouragement he needed: she was acting like a caricature of the down-to-business bed partners he had found so unfulfilling before he met her. Lydia was, in effect, asking him to do sex with her, not make love. She, too, it appeared, was frightened of intimacy.

Yet at the same time that Lydia was behaving provocatively, she was also castigating Marc for acting cold and withdrawn, for becoming a "sexual automaton." On the surface, it seems grossly unfair of her to make such a demand considering her own behavior, but I am sure that Lydia, too, was genuinely hungry for intimacy. After the intimate, sensuous lovemaking she had experienced with Marc at the beginning of their relationship, his withdrawal made her feel deprived, depressed, and frightened of losing him.

But pushing for intimacy—relentlessly nagging for it—*is a perfect way of making sure that your partner will never give it to you.* Like Pleasure Pushers, Intimacy Pushers are really pushing their partners away, and, at some level, I believe they know that. A man or woman who shouts "Open up to me!" or "Show me your feelings!" or "Be tender when you touch me!" is, in reality, practicing the oldest form of reverse psychology. Because I have yet to meet anyone who is moved to open up or be vulnerable or feel tender *on demand.* Opening up is a risky business and who wants to take risks with an aggressor? I frequently have the heretical thought that the reason why so many women nag their men for intimacy is because they are scared to death of it themselves and pushing for intimacy is a blameless (and tricky) way of avoiding it. Scratch the surface of a woman who is always shouting "Please open up to me!" and you just might find a closed and frightened person.

"I hate loving Marc more than he loves me," Lydia told me with tears in her eyes.

"Then back off and give him a chance to love you back," I said to her softly. "He'll never come out of the corner this way."

Lydia's fear of heartbreak was getting in the way of exactly what she wanted. Living with her constant terror of being abandoned made her so anxious that she rushed to make it a reality—in effect, to get it over with. In the end, her dread of heartbreak became her fear of intimacy; the only sure way she could avoid being hurt or disappointed by Marc was by retreating from her own feelings for him. But then she, too, was back where she started from just like Marc.

"It's Time to Take Action—
Sensuous Action"

Even after all these years of working with couples, I never cease to be amazed by the complicated ways people avoid simply feeling love for each other. The Marc and Lydia who arrived in my office were victims of their own and each other's fears of intimacy. He was cold and withdrawn; she was demanding and taunting. He suppressed his emotions to get through sex; she focused on sex to avoid risking heartbreak. They had once been a perfect match, and now they were a perfect mismatch. They were exactly the opposite of the loving couple they had once been and still longed to be.

My heart went out to these two. They had had a special relationship, full of love and pleasure, and they had sacrificed that love to their fears. If I had been dispensing conventional therapy, we would have talked for weeks, digging our way to the origins of their respective fears. And perhaps after a few months of introspection, Marc would have been prompted to verbally reassure Lydia that he was not about to give up on their relationship and Lydia would have been ready to promise Marc to try to be less demanding and "give him more space" in their relationship. But my guess was that Marc's words alone could never reach that place where Lydia felt her terror of abandonment, nor could Lydia's protestations begin to calm Marc's panic about drowning in their relationship.

"Words aren't going to work here," I told them. "It's time to take action—sensuous action."

The only way I know how to merge love and sex is to learn how to give and receive sensuous pleasure. It is the way we get our feelings back again and the way we can share those feelings with one another. I am not denying the spiritual elements of love, nor the mysteries of emotional chemistry, nor the complexities of psychological needs and defenses. But I still believe that love and sex intersect in a relationship when both partners are capable of relaxed, unthreatening, and undemanding sensuous pleasure. This is the point of primal connection, the point where all relatedness began. And it all begins with a touch.

It was perfectly clear to me that if Marc and Lydia were ever to get back to sensuous lovemaking and get their loving feelings flowing again, they had to stop doing sex immediately. Doing sex only made Marc feel lonely and guilty and it only fueled Lydia's fear that Marc was withdrawing from her. Enough. We had to cut through that Gordian entanglement in one fell swoop.

"But sex is the last link between us," Lydia protested.

"Right now it's not a link, it's a wedge," I replied. "It's the way you avoid intimacy. I want to get you back to making love and that means starting your love life all over again from scratch."

Making love was fraught with danger for this couple. It elicited feelings that made them feel helpless, anxious, and frightened. In order for them to get back to the marvelous pleasures, comfort, and intimacy it could give them, they had to stop feeling overwhelmed by those feelings.

"We're going to take it one step at a time," I told them. "And the moment you feel anxious, stop and go back three spaces. I want to *very slowly* bring you back to that place where you both feel safe being intimate with one another."

The Graduated Sensual Exercises reach to places words cannot touch. Instead of trying to untwist a complex pattern of unsatisfying behavior, I use the exercises to start behavior all over again. In order to learn how to merge love and sex, Marc needed first to experience his loving, sensual feelings *apart* from sex and *then* to experience holding on to those feelings as he moved very gradually into sexual arousal. Only then could Marc truly believe that he was in control of his feelings and only that way could he be rid of his panic about drowning in his emotions. Likewise, for Lydia to learn how to merge love and sex, she needed to ask

Marc directly to caress her—to give her pleasure—and *then* to have the experience of him *not disappearing* when she did. Only then could she truly believe that Marc would not abandon her if she let her own sensations and emotions run free. The steps of these exercises are slow and deceptively simple, but they reorganize a couple's behavior in powerful ways.

One therapist I know speaks of intimacy in terms of its sound-alike, "into-me-see." When you are intimate with your lover, you take the risk of letting him see you in perfect nakedness—exactly as you really are. No masking your feelings, not dressing up your physical reactions.

"Look!" you say. "This is who I am! This is how I really feel!"

At some point in the Graduated Sensual Exercises, I ask a couple to share the *ultimate secret* they have from each other: I ask them to go home and masturbate in tandem—separately, but in full view of each other. In Part II, we will discuss the formidable resistance most people have to trying this experiment. Lydia, like so many others, protested that she could think of nothing "more unromantic and impersonal."

"You can't get any more impersonal than you've already been with each other," I told her. "But it's time you started being *real* with each other."

Marc and Lydia needed to demystify each other in order to enjoy "into-me-see." Lydia needed to see Marc as a sexual being himself, not just her sexual mentor and savior. And Marc needed to see Lydia as capable of sexual self-sufficiency, not just as dependent and demanding of him. It took weeks before they could share this ultimate secret, but when they finally did, it was a momentous breakthrough for both of them.

"I thought the whole business was going to be tawdry and humiliating," Marc said later. "But it turned out to be incredibly liberating and moving. Lydia looked so innocent, so vulnerable to me. I felt so close to her, I just had to hold her."

In that moment, that "click," love and sex had merged for

these two. And it stayed that way. Over the next few weeks, as they continued through the remainder of the exercises, they drew closer and closer to one another. It was obvious that the magic was back; these two had fallen in love again.

"We don't feel that special intimacy every time we go to bed together," Lydia told me several months later. "Not even every other time. But it's like a touchstone that's always there in our relationship, even when we're screaming at each other. It's something we know we always will go back to."

"We don't have sex so much anymore," Marc interjected deadpan, then suddenly grinned. "But occasionally we do make love."

In Part I of this book, I've described some of the common ways we separate love from sex in our lives: how "speeding up" sex for efficiency's sake forces us to lose loving feelings; how gender roles, no matter how up-to-date and sophisticated, can still prevent us from risking emotional intimacy with our sexual partners; how the ancient deal of trading sex for love can leave both partners feeling cheated and lonely; how infidelity attempts to deal with our need for both love and sex by trying to satisfy these respective needs with different people, and how that attempt rarely succeeds.

In Part II, I will show how almost any couple who is willing to try can learn how to put love and sex back together again. No matter what the origin of that separation in a relationship, you can merge love and sex by getting in touch with your own and your partner's feelings in an entirely new way. Taking this step is always an emotional risk, but I have organized this program in such a way that the pleasures you receive always compensate for the "dangers" you encounter. And if you stick with it to the end, I am sure that you will have discovered that intimacy—emotional *and* sexual—that you have been looking for.

 PART II

How to Put the Love Back into Making Love

The Graduated Sensual Exercises

 *Chapter 9*

"Let's Skip This Part of the Book, Okay, Hon?"

We're going to start your sex life all over again.

"What?"

You heard me. We're going to start you over from scratch. As if you were an alien who had just slipped into a human's body and didn't know an orgasm from an orangeade. We're going to throw out everything that's ever worked for you—all the tried and true positions, all the familiar routines. In fact, for the next few weeks I want you to do nothing except follow the specific sensual regimen that I prescribe for you. And that means no sexual intercourse allowed until we get to the end of the program.

"Let's skip this part of the book, okay, hon?"

Look, I know all this scares you to death, but please don't skip it. Just give it a try. I promise you on a stack of self-help books that never worked that this one is going to make a difference. If you follow these simple Graduated Sensual Exercises, not only will your sex life ultimately expand in ways you never imagined it could, but you will awaken a whole spectrum of deep feelings that will flow between you. You are going to learn how to experience each part of lovemaking as a separate entity with a range of sensations and feelings that you have been missing for years. And you are going to learn how to fully enjoy these feelings free of anxieties. These are the feelings that intimate love is made of.

"Hold it, Dagmar! You're talking about those exercises where you take turns touching each other's bodies, right? Aren't they just for couples with serious sexual problems?"

No, these exercises are for everyone who wants to improve his or her love life. That's about 95 percent of the population, the way I figure it. True, many of the original concepts for these exercises come from Masters and Johnson's work with specific sexual dysfunctions, but over the years I have developed and adapted these exercises for *every* man and woman who simply wants to feel more sexually *and* emotionally in a relationship. And judging by the overwhelming results of my Sexual Expansion Workshops for "normal functioning" couples, these exercises work. Couples who could just do sex finally discovered the joys of making love.

But before we go on, there is something I ought to say about "serious sexual problems" and that is that I don't think they are all that different from the dissatisfactions that most "normal" people experience. A man who is a premature ejaculator is just a few steps farther down the line from a man who "functions" normally but is gradually losing his interest in making love; and a woman who is nonorgasmic is on the same continuum as a woman who is orgasmic but complains that she feels emotionally numb when she has sex with her husband. The symptoms vary, but what all these men and women have in common is that they are avoiding feelings—skipping past them or holding them back. The fact is that the woman who feels emotionally numb with her husband has at least as much to gain from the Graduated Sensual Exercises as the woman who cannot have orgasms in intercourse.

"Hey, but I'm perfectly happy with my sex life just the way it is."

That's just wonderful—especially if you are being absolutely honest with yourself. But don't you ever find yourself wondering if you aren't missing out on something in your love life? Some element of sensuality? Intimacy? Romance? Passion? All those emotions that run deeper than mere genital thrills? Something that separates making love from merely doing sex?

"Look, you can always imagine things better than the way they are, but I've given up on torturing myself with romantic dreams of perfect sex or of a profoundly intimate relationship. I'm a realist now. That's a sign of maturity, right?"

It sounds more like a sign of resignation than maturity. In fact, I'm convinced you are settling for less than you deserve—and truly want. Listen, is it really so horrible to admit to yourself, and to each other, that your love life could be better than it is right now? Isn't that the reason you picked up this book in the first place?

"Okay, so things could be better—especially in the bedroom department. But our problems aren't going to disappear just by giving each other back rubs. They're a lot more complex than that. We've got layers of anger to deal with first. We've got volumes to talk out before we can start making love again with any feeling."

Maybe. But my guess is that you've been talking things out for months, even years, and it is not getting you any closer together. The fact is that you could probably cut through a lot of your problems if you *stopped* talking and *started* touching. I know that sounds simplistic, like some dreamy panacea from the touchy-feely sixties, but the fact is, it works.

One couple came to me after seeing an even half-dozen psychotherapists and family therapists over as many years. These two fought about almost everything, from who'll do the dishes to what American policy should be in Central America. Once a week they had intercourse just before going to sleep—quickly and with the lights out—but the only feeling the act generated between them was more alienation. The next morning they would virtually start the day fighting again. I told them that the central tenet of my program was to "shut up and get undressed."

"It went against everything we believed in," the wife, Adrianne, said later. "Luke and I are verbal people. We firmly believed that if you talked about any problem long enough you'd find a solution. But nothing else had worked. We were just desperate and worn out enough to try something new, simpleminded as it sounded."

After only two weeks of *silent* Sensual Exercises, this pair discovered that they had virtually stopped fighting, especially about trivial matters.

"It turned our whole world upside-down," Luke told me. "Now it seems like all those years of yackety-yacking were our way of avoiding feeling anything for each other. An armor of words. Well, there's no armor left when you're just naked and silent."

I don't want to deny the value of open verbal communication for a couple, but I am convinced that nonverbal, sensual therapy taps into a dimension of communication that no amount of jabbering can provide. Instead of relentlessly telling each other, "You aren't sensitive to my needs" and "You don't give me enough space" and "We just aren't on the same wavelength," you regress to the primordial communication of touch. Then, amazingly, the feelings that flow between you suddenly transcend everything you have been accusing each other of.

Not long ago, my practice shared a waiting room with a psychotherapist who also treated couples. One day he came into my office and announced that we had a problem. He said that *my* patients were upsetting *his* patients.

"How?" I asked.

"A lot of your patients actually *neck* out there," he said, gesturing with annoyance to the waiting room. "They can't keep their hands off each other. And that makes my patients feel terribly inadequate. By the time they drag themselves into my office they're more depressed than ever because most of them haven't been affectionate with each other in months."

"What a shame," I replied. "But let's look on the bright side: maybe my couples will inspire yours."

Most couples find themselves becoming increasingly affectionate with each other after only two or three weeks of the Graduated Sensual Exercises. Whereas they used to sit side by side in front of the TV barely touching, now they sit hand in hand, arm across shoulder, head in lap. And whereas they used to curl up to sleep on opposite sides of the bed, now they lie curled up together, belly to back, leg across hip, head against shoulder. The truth is that when couples start touching one another, they almost immediately start liking each other better, and the more they like each other, the more they want to touch each other. It's a delicious cycle.

"Our bodies became such good friends that they wouldn't let us fight with each other anymore," one woman told me with a laugh at the end of her and her husband's second week of exercises.

That is precisely how the program works. As sensual contact begins to develop warmth and affection between you, your anger starts to melt, your recriminations become irrelevant, and your guilt evaporates.

"I'm not sure I want my anger to 'melt.' It's real and I don't want to cover it up with some phony lovey-dovey exercise."

You mean, your anger is like an old friend and you don't want to give it up. I can understand that. But these exercises don't *deny* your anger. You can still have the same gripes, the same 'unfinished business' when you get out of bed. The exercises just give you both the opportunity to experience what it is like to be together in a loving mode. It is like a reminder of what life together could be like and why you want it to get better.

"This is starting to sound a little simplistic, Dagmar. If it's so easy for

*couples to make this marvelous connection through these exercises, why doesn't
everybody do them?"*

If I had my way, everybody would. But as you can see for
yourself, just getting people to start is a formidable task. In my
private practice, I often have couples who come back to me week
after week without ever getting down to doing these exercises at
home. I tell them that they are wasting their money, that what
goes on in my office means nothing if they don't do their homework, and still they put it off. People would rather talk *ad nauseam*
about their problems than simply get undressed and touch each
other. Look, you yourself aren't quite ready to take that leap of
faith and try my program, are you?

*"Well, you've got to admit there is something nerdy about getting undressed
and getting into bed without any intention of actually making love. The whole
prospect feels juvenile and silly and more than a little bit humiliating."*

Listen, feeling juvenile is half the fun. It's the first step in
getting rid of all those unspoken rules and regulations that surround your "mature" love life as it is now, all that grown-up
rigidity that has made your relationship grow stale. Maybe you
have to risk feeling like a nerd to get something new going on in
your life.

But my guess is that there is something more fundamental
than fear of nerdiness holding you back, and it is the same thing
that inhibits most people from simply jumping in and trying my
program: *I think you are afraid that these exercises are actually going to
work!*

At some preconscious level, you are afraid that if your feelings
actually start flowing, if you really begin to feel intimately connected to each other, you are going to lose all control of your life.
You are afraid that once you crack open that dam that has been
restraining your feelings, you are going to drown in those feelings. You are afraid that if you totally relax under your partner's
touch, you will lose all your power in the relationship. You are

afraid that if you finally do let go, you will feel like a quivering, crying, helpless baby.

The fact is, that very panic lies just below the surface in *all* of us. *There is a child who longs to be endlessly caressed and petted inside every one of us*—inside every One Minute husband and wife, inside every Tough Guy and every Superwoman. And for most of us, that child has been denied so long, and those longings have become so great, that the very prospect of gently contacting that child overwhelms us. We are terrified that once released we will forever be that child.

But the truth is we *won't* be overwhelmed. And that is the wonder of the Graduated Sensual Exercises. This regimen is constructed in such a way that we always remain in control of our feelings and never become a victim of them. The reason the exercises are graduated—that we take in gradually increased levels of sensuality—is so that we can acclimatize ourselves to these feelings by degrees. Thus we discover that we can touch the child within each of us while always feeling confident that we will remain powerful and independent adults. It is only with that confidence that we can get all our feelings flowing. And once all our feelings are flowing, we will feel more alive, more whole, more in love than most of us have been in a very long time. That's how powerful this program is.

"I don't have the faintest idea what you are talking about, Dagmar. All this 'child within' stuff sounds like psychobabble to me. If I have a child inside me who longs to be touched, I haven't heard so much as a burp from him in years. And if I'm unconsciously afraid that I'll go off the deep end if my partner gives me a belly rub, I'm crazier than I ever imagined. I mean, at my age I think I can handle it."

That's terrific. Then there's nothing stopping you from trying the first Graduated Sensual Exercise.

"Hold it. I need a few more details before I commit myself to anything. Like how much time is this thing going to take?"

Each individual touching session lasts from fifteen minutes to three-quarters of an hour. But each session is really a *double* session because you take turns being the Toucher and the Touchee, so that means that each double session will take from a half hour to an hour and a half. And to get the most out of the program, you have to allow yourselves three double sessions a week for the next six weeks.

"You've got to be kidding, Dagmar. One and a half hours three times a week for the next month and a half? Who's got the time for this stuff besides rich matrons and retirees? We've got jobs, children, a household to run. Do you really expect me to drop everything so I can play rub-a-dub-dub with my spouse? Give me a break."

It always comes down to time, doesn't it? These days nobody seems to think that they can afford an hour and a half every other day just for their own "pointless pleasure."

"By the time I hit the sack, I've been going nonstop for seventeen, eighteen hours," one woman protested when I outlined the program to her and her husband. "I don't have the energy for anything that's going to take an hour and a half."

"But then why are you here?" I asked her.

"You know very well why," she answered with a scowl. "Because we hardly ever make love anymore."

Incredible!

Couple after couple tell me that by the time they get to bed they are too tired to do anything with each other—let alone a "big production" like the Sensual Exercises. And in the next breath they want to know what the secret is to a more satisfying love life?

But what have these couples done before bedtime? Gone out to dinner with friends? A cocktail party? The theater? The movies? How many hours and a half have they spent out socializing with colleagues and friends.

"What are we supposed to do, become hermits for the next six weeks? We'll drop out of circulation in no time. People will get hurt feelings if we start

turning down that many invitations. We're going to run out of excuses pretty quick."

You can always tell your friends that you two have decided to spend more time alone together—in bed.

"Get serious."

Well, then how about telling your friends something more socially acceptable, like that you need more time for your work?

While we're at it, let's take a look at what else you do between dinner and dropping off exhausted into bed. Statistically speaking, there is a good chance that you spend at least an hour either reading the newspaper or watching the news on TV. It never ceases to amaze me how many people insist that they feel "unfulfilled" if they miss the latest news before going to bed—it's as if watching the news were their way of controlling the world. What impresses me, of course, is that ultimately what these people are telling me is that watching the news is more fulfilling than sex and love are. At least that is the way they have set up their priorities.

Not to mention just plain old recreational TV. The statistics on the average time spent watching TV—including films on the VCR—as compared to time spent making love are truly remarkable, particularly when you consider how many of the films and programs watched are so sexually oriented. We seem to think nothing of watching a two-hour film loaded with sexy scenes, yet the prospect of an hour and a half spent sensually touching one another seems a gross imposition on our schedules. Would we really rather watch other people making love than do it ourselves?

"You're really trying to shame me into trying your program, aren't you, Dagmar?"

Not shame you. Just trying to help get your priorities in order. As a matter of fact, now is a good time for you to draw up a list of your priorities. Where does time for sex and sensuality rank on your schedule now? And where would it rank ideally? Be honest. Don't put sex at number one if you know very well that time for work and the children takes precedence over it. But on the other hand, pay close attention to where you rank time for "pointless pleasure" in relation to your social life and your recreational life. Do you really want sensual time together to be less important in your life than Tom Brokaw and "L.A. Law," jogging and aerobics, putting in the tulip bulbs and chopping wood, shiatsu massage and yoga classes?

Maybe it will help you establish new priorities if you stop thinking of the Sensual Exercises as a tiring and tiresome duty. Yes, they can be anxiety-producing at first, but very soon they become tranquilizing, not tiring, fascinating, not tiresome. And now comes the truly ironic part of my job: I am actually going to try to sell you on sensuality by listing some of its "side benefits." Only in the eighties!

The truth is, the Graduated Sensual Exercises will provide you with many of the very benefits you are seeking in your various "de-stressing" activities. They help relieve all stress, not just sexual anxieties. As well as any yoga class or professional massage, these exercises relax you, take you away from your preoccupations with work and personal problems. The immediate concrete results are the same as those derived from other de-stressing pursuits too: you will sleep better and need less of it, have fewer headaches and colds. And here is the kicker: if you make lingering sensuality a continuing part of your life, chances are *you will live longer!* (How's that for ultimate efficiency? You will actually *gain* time.) I am quite serious. It has been well established that stress increases the risk for killer heart and vascular diseases and that, therefore, reducing stress reduces that risk. But there is also a growing body of evidence that shows that human touch in particular has life-extending qualities. Years ago, the famous Fels study of orphaned infants demonstrated that babies who were regularly fondled had a much lower incidence of infant mortality than babies who were never fondled at all. Recent studies imply that the same is true for adults: married people live longer than single people; even people with pets live longer than people without "something to pet." All of which is to say that you can afford to give up the health club and yoga class, even a day or two of jogging, to spend a few hours each week in pursuit of pointless pleasure with your spouse.

In the next chapter we'll talk about how to schedule your time for these exercises so that you do not have children or undo fatigue to contend with, but for now suffice it to say that the time is there if you want it. And that, really, is half the reason for committing yourself to these three double sessions per week. This in itself is an exercise in "making time" for your relationship. Let's face it, there is no way you are ever going to make unhurried love even *once* a week if you are unwilling to make time for it.

"All right, already, I'm convinced. I'll give your exercises a try. But my commitment is worthless—unless, of course, I'm going to do these exercises alone. Because you see, I'll never get Bozo to do them with me."

Ah yes, the Bozo factor (sometimes known as the Lulu factor). It comes up with almost every couple. One wants to try the exercises but the other thinks it's a waste of time, or worse, that it's just asking for trouble. He (or she) will say that he is perfectly happy with his love life just the way it is. And then, when you volunteer that *you* aren't perfectly happy with it, when you tell him that you've lost some of your sense of adventure and romance, that lately you have been feeling a little numb and estranged when you have sex together, he may very well become deeply hurt.

He'll blurt out, "You mean you don't like sex with me anymore? You don't like the way I do it?"

And you'll have to answer: "It's not sex that's the problem. It's feelings I'm talking about. It feels like we're doing sex but not really making love anymore. And these exercises are supposed to be a way of getting those feelings back, so I want to try them."

And then he'll probably get very angry: "This sounds like your problem, not mine. Why don't you go fix it by yourself."

And then you really have no choice. Because you are hardly the one to tell him (or her) that he is probably just as stuck as you are, that deep inside he probably longs for a change in your relationship, too—that if he were honest with himself he would find that he, too, wishes he felt more when he made love and he, too, wishes he were more sensual, and that nothing is going to change unless he tries something as new and radical as the Sensual Exercises. No, these are not things that you can tell your spouse. Or, put another way, these are not things that your spouse will *hear* you tell him. So, you tell him something else which is equally true but infinitely more acceptable.

You say: "Just do it for me, honey. I can't do these exercise alone. I need your help. Please."

"What? Humiliate myself like that? No way! I'm not going to beg him. I mean, what if he says, 'Okay, I'll do the damned exercises, but only for you.' "

Then you're in luck. You say thank you. You can even tell him that he can do the exercises and hate them—as long as he promises to do them. Because I assure you, he will not hate them for long. And what you have to understand is that there is a good chance that the only way he can get himself to try these exercises is by telling himself that he is "doing you a favor." Otherwise *he* would feel too humiliated and foolish to try them. The bottom line is, you are now both ready to commit yourselves to a remarkable adventure.

Almost. Because undoubtedly there will be other alibis and delays to overcome before you actually put this commitment in action. The first usually runs something like this:

"Okay, I'll do the exercises, but now is a bad time. I mean, you can see for yourself that I'm smack in the middle of a high-pressure period. Why don't we wait until vacation to start this regime. I mean, we'll both be more in the mood then anyhow, right, hon?"

To which you reply: "Wrong, hon. You've been in the middle of this high-pressure period for as long as I can remember. In fact, I think that's part of our problem. All I'm asking for is a maximum of four and a half hours a week and those hours are going to take some of the pressure off, not put more on. Let's just jump in and do it, okay?"

Now you are both just about ready to begin. And this is usually the point when Bozo makes one last attempt to pull the rug out from under the whole project:

"I hope you understand that I am only committed to trying these exercises once, honey."

And you say: "Great. How about right now?"

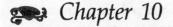 ***Chapter 10***

"I Want to Be Touched Now"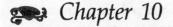

Week One

Start with a flip of a coin.

The winner gets to be the first Touchee, the one who initiates the first sensuous exercise, the one who gets to be touched first.

Listen, you might as well do this right now. Strike while the commitment is hot. Set this book down for a second and flip the old coin so that as you read on you know who's who: who's first Toucher and who's first Touchee.

And here is what the winner of the toss does: sometime within the next week she (or he) must say out loud, "I want to be touched now." And then she should take her partner by the hand and lead him up to the bedroom. There, both of you undress with the lights on and crawl into bed. And don't forget to take the phone off the hook.

From now until the session is over, you are going to enter a world focused entirely on sensation. No talk until you are finished—not a word. Your whole purpose, whether you are the Toucher or the Touchee, is to concentrate on what you are feeling in your body and in your heart.

For the next fifteen to forty-five minutes—Touchee's choice—Toucher, touch your partner's body all over with the exception of breasts (that includes male breasts) and genitals. Otherwise, try to cover as much territory as you possibly can, scalp to toes. Touchee, just lie there as relaxed as you can, drinking it all in, and *resist the temptation to touch back.* You'll have your turn next. And remember both of you, no matter what comes up—literally or figuratively—stick to the rules: no genital stimulation, no intercourse, no orgasms allowed. You're taking a vacation from that for a little while. You'll have a whole lifetime to do whatever you want later.

When the Touchee gives the signal, it's time to switch roles—Toucher becomes Touchee and vice versa. No coffee breaks. Do not pass Go. Just switch places and experience sensations from the other point of view.

Those are the basics for your first session. Don't talk about it afterward, no critiques or postmortems, just pull on your socks and get on with your normal lives. But remember, sometime in the remaining days of this first week it is your partner's turn to be the Initiator, to get another double session rolling with the announcement, "I want to be touched now." Before the end of the week, switch again so that you initiate your third and final double session for this first week.

"That's it, Dagmar? That's your big secret to love and sex? Two people take turns touching each other while scrupulously avoiding the Big Spots and presto-chango, they become intimate, sensuous lovers? Come on, all that will come of that is a load of frustration. Or is that your whole point? You're trying to get us to have the longest foreplay in history so that by the time we're allowed to do the real thing we'll be so grateful that we'll finally do it right?"

There is no "doing it right." Making love is not a performance or gymnastic event. There is only *feeling.* And that is what these exercises are all about. Not foreplay—this touching is not leading up to anything. *It is a fantastic pleasure in its own right.* And simpleminded as that may sound, yes, that *is* one of my 'big secrets' to love and sex.

Just setting yourself a minimum of fifteen minutes apiece for sheer passive pleasure allows you to start acquiring that fine art known as Lingering with Sensuality. But for people used to squeezing sex into a tight schedule, it can be the challenge of their lives.

"It felt like purgatory," one man told about his first session as Touchee. "After five minutes, I kept looking at the clock counting the seconds until I could finally tell her to stop."

This was a man who over the years had managed to squeeze most of the sensuality out of his love life. For him, the bottom line had always been orgasms—one for him and one for his wife —before he rolled over and squeezed in a few hours sleep. He was an efficiency expert at doing sex: he could finish the whole "job" in under fifteen minutes. How was he going to "endure" this touching business for fifteen minutes?

"Close your eyes and forget the clock," I told him. "There are no goals today, so you're stuck with just the sensations you can feel now. You might as well make the most of them."

For the next three sessions this man suffered through the ordeal of being touched for fifteen minutes with his eye still glued to the clock. But the fourth session, something happened.

"It was like this switch was pulled inside of me," he said. "And all of a sudden I was feeling these fantastic sensations in my chest and belly and thighs. It was like getting high. And when I opened my eyes, I saw that I'd been lost in this thing for forty-five minutes."

The "switch" that was pulled was his focus. He was finally allowing himself to focus on what was happening to him *now* instead of on when it was going to be over.

Our reluctance to stay in the Sensual Here and Now is the cause of most of our sexual dissatisfactions. Anxiety-filled "deadline sex" can rush some men into becoming premature ejaculators and force some women to "give up" trying for orgasm. But time-pressured deadline sex also takes its toll on those of us who "function normally" yet still feel emotionally short-changed, numb in the heart, and lonely as we rush through doing sex. That is why the sensuous exercises work for all of us, whatever our dissatisfaction. The secret for everyone is to focus on what you are feeling *now* without being rushed and without anticipating the next step. In Alcoholics Anonymous and Al-Anon, they tell you to focus on living one day at a time. In this program, I want you to focus on one sensation at a time. You will be astounded at the difference it will make.

"Come on, Dagmar, you act like all we've ever done is slam-bang, impersonal sex and that's simply not true. We always touch each other for a while before we go at it."

But do you really linger with the sensuality? Do you ever slow down so much that you don't have a thought of where any of this is leading? Do you ever get to the point where you are so fixed in the moment that the sensation you are feeling right now is all there is in the world?

"What is this, Dagmar, sensual therapy or Zen Buddhism? You make it sound so mystical—and so awfully artificial, too."

Well, there is something mystical about it; I'll grant you that. Ultimately, the reason why caressing your partner's body can elicit so many profound feelings is an exquisite mystery. In part, of course, it is because caresses awaken memories of parental touches from our early childhood, but does that explain why touch itself is so powerful?

But I refuse to accept your claim that my approach to sensuality is artificial. On the contrary, I think these exercises will bring you back to the most natural and fundamental way of relating to each other. Lingering sensuality is what's natural. Unfortunately, it has been socialized right out of our skins by a goal-oriented society, by insecure egos preoccupied with sexual performance, and by pop notions of erotic fulfillment which keep us so fixated on our genitalia that we forget we have hearts and bodies, too.

"All right, already, I get your point. But you have to admit that you're overreacting when you insist that we don't touch breasts or genitals. Now that's artificial—and more than a little perverse, too."

I'm not overreacting, I'm overcompensating for years of numbing and isolating habits. Like I said at the beginning, we're starting your sex life all over again. And the first step is to sensitize your *entire body*—not just your genitals.

"I had this incredible memory flash while Bob was softly caressing the inside of my arm and the palm of my hand," one wife told me. "I flashed on the first time a boy took my hand at a dance in junior high. I remember it felt like electricity shooting through me. It's not the kind of thrill an old married lady gets anymore."

"It sounds to me like you just had it again," I told her. "And that's just the beginning."

By skipping breasts and genitals in the first stage of this program, you give the rest of your body a chance to catch up. It is high time you got the idea out of your head that these holy spots are the only sexual parts of your body. We're going to give your genitals a rest for a while. They simply can't do everything for you, can't be the repository of all your sensations, can't be your heart and soul. As you gradually relax the controls that numb the rest of your body, you will start to feel sensitive everywhere. Soon you are going to have erotic elbows and passionate eyelids, rapturous kneecaps and sensuous earlobes. You are going to be one head-to-toe erogenous zone. And that, I swear, *is* natural.

"Terrific. But let me tell you what is artificial—this business of making such a production number out of initiating the session. 'I want to be touched now.' Really! What happened to spontaneity and subtlety? What happened to romance?"

You mean, what happened to the guessing game of, 'I wonder if she's in the mood to do it now?' And what happened to the negotiations of, 'Last time you wanted to do it and I didn't, but if you'll do it this time when you don't want to and I do, then next time . . .'? And what happened to those tentative signals you used to send each other (usually under the bedcovers with your toes when you were both half asleep) which were purposely ambiguous so that no response did not have to be taken as a personal rejection?

Well, all that "subtlety" and "spontaneity" and "romance" is just going to have to stay on hold for a few weeks while you replace it with the most direct and conscious communication I can think of: "Now. I want to be touched now."

"I protested like crazy when you told us to do that 'Touch me now' business," one husband confided to me. "But secretly I was relieved."

It had been over three months since this man and his wife had made love.

"We ended up in this 'layoff' after Rhea [his wife] refused me three times in a row," he went on. "I couldn't take another rejection, so I just stopped asking."

And, of course, his wife never asked either. An unspoken rule of their relationship was that she could never initiate lovemaking, a fact that she had begun to resent. So there they were, both stuck. We spent some time discussing their respective fears and resentments, but I knew the best way to unstick them was by "artificially" changing the rules in one fell swoop. I told them to take turns initiating touching each other, no questions asked. Not subtle, maybe not even romantic at this point, but it was infinitely more satisfying than what they were doing—or rather, *not* doing—now.

For many couples, simply getting sex started is a formidable problem. Weeks, even months can go by with nothing happening because He is afraid She will reject him again or She is afraid that He will find her too aggressive so She keeps looking for ways to get Him to think it's his idea. Or He is so afraid that He will not be potent that He would rather not try. Or She is so afraid that She will take forever to come that She would rather not try. Or both are waiting so desperately for that magical moment when they will fly into each other's arms, rip off each other's clothes, and fall hungrily into bed, that any urge short of that seems too puny to do anything about. The list of reasons we develop for *not* getting started is endless. So for the next few weeks, we are simply going to throw that list out.

There is only one reason why you are going to get started three times during this coming week: *because that is the deal you are making with each other.*

And no, it is not subtle to stand up after the ten o'clock news and declare that right now you want to be touched. It is exactly the opposite: it is direct, assertive, and, scariest of all, it is *conscious.* Sex isn't just "happening" due to circumstances beyond your control; you are taking *responsibility* for making it happen. You are admitting to yourself and declaring to your partner that you want him to give you pleasure and you want him to do it right now. That may seem crude and unfeminine and unromantic, but believe me, it ultimately makes you feel wonderful about yourself and your sexuality. Even though it is just an exercise and you are only "following Dagmar's rules," this open declaration of your desire is a gigantic step toward bringing sex and love under your own control. Waiting time is over; you are now going after your own pleasure.

And not only does your demand make sex conscious, it also makes it selfish—in the very best sense of that word. When you reach across the couch to take your partner by the hand, you are not even pretending that there is anything "mutual" about your urge or its timing. You are saying, "I want you to do something for me now," not, "I want to do something for you now." This puts an end to all guessing games: it really does not matter whether your partner is in the mood or not—that's not a part of this deal. You are going to take turns initiating these sessions over the next few weeks and *that* is perfectly mutual, perfect equality. You are about to embark on the most splendid vacation of your life together: *a vacation from worrying about what your partner wants and feels.*

Finally, you can also stop letting any fears of sexual failure get in your way of initiating these sessions. During these early stages, erections and lubrication, orgasms and heavy breathing are all totally irrelevant. You can't fail because all performances have been canceled. If you have an orgasm when he caresses your back, wonderful; and if you get an erection when she massages your thighs, fine. But that's not your goal; it's just a side effect.

"Great. So I consciously and selfishly declare that I want to be touched now. That means it's going to be doubly humiliating when he says no."

But he cannot say no. That's the bottom line of this program: no no's allowed. When both of you committed yourselves to trying these exercises, you committed yourselves to always being there for your partner. Absolutely and with no questions asked.

Sticking to this part of the deal is crucial. When your partner says, "Now," you can not say, "Not tonight, I'm exhausted" or "Won't you take a rain check? I've got to finish the Bailey report by tomorrow" or "But I've been looking forward to the football game all day long." In fact, you can't even say, "Why don't we wait until later when we'll be getting undressed for bed anyhow?"

If you're not unconscious, you can do it. You don't have to do it right or even do it well. You just have to do it.

"Okay, so I did it!" one husband, Ron, growled at me at the end of his first week with the exercises. "I was a good boy. But, damn it, I resented every second of it. I'm not going to lie to you. I mean, Teri came waltzing up to my desk and said, 'Let's rub tummies now,' when she knew damned well that I had to have a report done by morning. Now if you think that's the way to turn me into a loving husband, you're even crazier than I thought."

"And how do you think I felt knowing that he was resenting the whole deal?" his wife, Teri, cried reproachfully. "How was I supposed to enjoy myself while he was in a rotten mood?"

Fortunately, they were both blaming me rather than each other —a step forward in their relationship. As a therapist, some of my best work is done being a punching bag. But still, there was something I had to remind these two about their relationship as it existed before anyone ever mentioned Sensual Exercises.

"What used to happen when Teri wanted to make love and you thought you were too busy?" I asked Ron.

"Well, I'd just very reasonably explain to her that I was under pressure and the timing wasn't good and I'd make it up to her later," Ron replied.

"And how would that make you feel?" I asked Teri, already knowing the answer by the expression on her face.

"Rotten!" she said. "Like some little girl who's being patronized. And anyway, he's always under pressure. I can't remember that last time that the timing was good."

Over the years, I think I have heard just about every conceivable variation on "Not tonight, dear" and not one of them opens the door for very much intimacy.

There's the direct, but petulant refusal: "What's the matter with you? Are you obsessed or something? All you think about is sex."

And there's the best-defense-is-a-good-offense refusal: "You've sure got a knack for picking the exact wrong moment for these things, don't you?"

And then, of course, there is the martyr's acceptance which is tantamount to a refusal: "Okay, if you need it that badly."

In this program you cut through that whole morass of guilts and resentments. It's a deal, pure and simple: I'll be there for you, if you'll be there for me. Quid pro quo. As I told Ron, that pledge is the quickest route to intimacy I know of. It's a pledge of trust, of a willingness to please each other, and artificial as it may sound at this point, it makes you both feel more clear and comfortable with each other than a whole year's anguished discussions of who gives more to whom.

Ron still wasn't convinced.

"Great. But I'm still going to feel resentful following her up to the bedroom when I've got a deskful of work to do," he said.

"Fine. Resent away," I told him. "But do yourself a favor and don't hang on to your resentment if you happen to feel it fading away as you find yourself enjoying Teri's caresses. And later on, if you happen to notice that there's something refreshing about being rid of all that gamesmanship that used to surround initiating sex in your house, give a little smile, would you?"

But Ron wasn't smiling now and neither was Teri.

"I don't see how anything's going to change," she said. "I'm still going to feel rotten and guilty knowing he'd rather be doing his work than be in bed with me. Where's the pleasure in that for me?"

"The pleasure is still there," I told her. "You just have to allow yourself to accept it. It sounds to me like you are so devoted to being the pleasing person in this relationship that you've forgotten how to please yourself."

And then I told Teri something that she found very hard to believe: "You are actually going to get more out of these exercises if you can say 'I want to be touched now' at times when you *know* Ron doesn't want to. I know that sounds terribly perverse. But at this point, that's exactly the kind of practice you need. You have to challenge yourself to block out *his* needs so that you can finally focus on your own feelings."

For all of you who commit to these exercises, that is your only obligation—to focus on what you are feeling. Push away all thoughts of how your partner feels about touching you, whether he is enjoying it, if he finds you attractive, whether he is getting tired. When you think about those things, you distract your attention from your own sensations. Above all, don't bring your session to an end because you think he is bored or tired of touching you. Take your full forty-five minutes if that's what you want. And if your partner only took the minimum fifteen minutes when he was Touchee, do not let that influence how long you take when it's your turn to be Touchee. Take as much pleasure as you can bear for as long as you want.

"You know, I can already see how this is going to work out. I'll finally get up my nerve and I'll initiate the first double session. And then it will be his turn to initiate the next session—and it won't happen. Nothing. The whole week will go by without him so much as nodding toward the bedroom door."

Let's worry about that at the end of the week. He just might surprise you. But in the meantime, a cardinal rule of this program is that you cannot nudge him at all. You cannot so much as remind him that he's running out of time. Not a peep, not even if it's ten to midnight on the last day of the week. No Pleasure Pushing allowed. That would break down the whole structure of shared responsibility which you are starting to build here. Just make sure that you initiate that first session and that you get as much out of it as you can.

"This is all fascinating in theory, Dagmar, but let's finally get practical, shall we? Our seven-year-old is a light sleeper and our twelve-year-old doesn't go to bed until eleven. When are we supposed to do these exercises—between two and three in the morning?"

If necessary, yes. In fact, you are even allowed to wake your partner up in the middle of the night and say, "Now. I want to be touched now."

"And he'll say, 'Now. I want to get divorced now.'"

No he won't. Because he has the right to do the very same thing next time. Again, I don't want to sound totally perverse, but both of you will find it positively exhilarating to see just how far you can push this thing. Go ahead, wake him up in the middle of the night and say, "Now." And you, stick your head into the shower and say to her, "Now." Push the limits. See for yourself how giddy-making it is to play I'll-Be-There-For-You-If-You'll-Be-There-For-Me.

But yes, there is a practical side to this program which you should consider at this point. If children keep you from having the privacy you need for these exercises (as they may have kept you from having a rich love life in the past), it's time you made some new arrangements. First, if you haven't done it already, put a lock on your bedroom door. And why don't you get a baby-sitter and rent a hotel room for one of the sessions? You're willing to treat yourself to dinner and a movie, why does it seem any more self-indulgent to spend the same money (and use the same baby-sitter) for some pointless sensual pleasure? And anyway, what's wrong with being self-indulgent? Who else were you supposed to indulge today? Later on in the program, when sensual lovemaking has become a central part of your lives, the option of "sexing out" at hotels and motels will probably be high on your list of things to do on a night out.

And here's an idea that is so obvious it's a wonder so few of us ever think of it: you can actually initiate a sensuous exercise (or later, make love) *during the day.* That's right, you can roll in the hay while the sun shines, instead of always thinking that you have to make hay. Say on a Saturday, instead of raking the leaves, or on a Sunday, instead of reading the paper from cover to cover. Get your kids a play date and have one of your own with your bedmate. Too many people only think of making love when they are already undressed and in bed for sleep. The idea of deliberately taking off our clothes just to give each other pleasure seems positively scandalous. But scandalous is wonderful! In fact, the more scandalous and illicit it feels to you, the better. It's time you broke out of your old routines. It's time you felt a little decadent. It can only help you to feel more sensual.

It's the deliberateness of undressing in the middle of the day that inhibits us. When you start stripping at two in the afternoon, you can no longer kid yourself into thinking that this sensual interlude is "just happening." No, you are making it happen. You are doing it because you want the pleasure of it. God knows, it is easier for most of us to take off our clothes in the middle of the afternoon to change for a set of tennis than it is to strip for some sensuous fun. Interestingly, couples tell me that they frequently get turned on when they are undressing for tennis but, sadly, they rarely follow through on their impulse—after all, the court is reserved, people are waiting. But this Saturday afternoon nothing is waiting; only your bodies.

While I'm at it, let me throw in a couple more practical details. There's nothing worse than a cold room for the sensual exercises. It simply does not feel the same when it all has to be done under the comforter. For one, the Toucher usually ends up feeling suffocated. I suggest you invest in a portable heater that will live in your bedroom. Turn it on the minute you know you are going to initiate a sensuous session. (In fact, you might want to turn it on an hour ahead of time.) Now you can both lie on the bed naked, uncovered, and un-goose-bumped for the entire double session.

Some couples also like to add music and scented candles to the bedroom for the occasion. Fine. Later, we'll talk more about the accoutrements of the sensuous household. But for now, just remember that the Touchee decides everything: if there is going to be music and what kind, candles or no. The Touchee is totally in charge of his or her own experience.

"Once we're undressed and she's lying on the bed, what am I supposed to do? (the Toucher asks). *Give her some kind of health club massage?"*

Touch her any way you want—fingertip caresses here, gentle kneading of tense muscles there—and trust that if she wants anything different she will let you know. The Touchee is always your guide. She will show you how hard, how fast, and how long she wants to be touched. It's her responsibility entirely, so you do not have to worry about doing it wrong.

You are not supposed to become some kind of expert at this. You don't have to bone up on the "art of sensuous massage" or on Shiatsu meridians. It's your instincts I want you to get in touch with, not another technique. As far as I'm concerned, "technique" has been the death of real sensuality in our time. There are so many ideas bandied about that tell us that this newly discovered spot is the secret to the ultimate turn-on, that if you tone up your vaginal muscles here or rub this cream there, push this way or pull that way, you will unlock the gates to super sexuality. Somewhere along the line we have been bamboozled into thinking that we are nothing more than a series of computer buttons that have to be pushed in the right sequence to produce the jackpot: the Super Orgasm. I don't believe a word of it.

First, we are just too different from one another for this to be true: one person's G-spot is another person's "Zzzz spot." Our bodies not only vary in their sensitivities from one another, they also vary from day to day. One day your partner's feet may be particularly responsive, the next day it's the nape of her neck. That is why you always have to be guided by your partner. No therapist or book can tell you where to touch and when; only your partner can. And remember, you are not searching for her erotic hot spots anyhow. You are not trying to produce arousal or orgasms. You are eliciting a whole spectrum of sensations and the emotions that flow from them.

The other reason I eschew "technique" is because I want you to turn your rational mind off for a while so that you can go with your irrational impulses. For once, let your fingers follow your feelings instead of following a mental diagram of where you think the "perfect lover" should be touching her. Because here is the real secret: you, the Toucher, are going to get something sensual out of this experience, too. You are not simply the "robot" masseur at your partner's service; you are not solely tuned in to her responses. You've got sensitivities in your hand, too. Do you remember as a teenager that sensation of reaching under your girlfriend's sweater and touching her belly with the palm of your hand? It was electric. That thrill shot through your whole body. Now you are going to get that thrill back.

"So I only touch her with my hands?"

This first week, yes. Next week you can get more creative, as you'll see. But for now, just touch your partner with your hands and resist playing a game of tic-tac-toe on her back or drawing pictures on her buttocks—this can be a way of avoiding feeling anything. And no tickling; that's about the most antisensual thing you can do. Relax, but don't become immobilized. There's a tendency for Touchers to plop themselves down on their side on one elbow and remain in the same position for the entire session. That way you only cover what's in between knees and neck, a real shame considering that her head and feet may be very sensitive that day. Move around. Get out of the bed and walk to her other side. Turn around and face her feet. It won't wear you out.

"And what am I supposed to do? (the Touchee asks). *Lie there like a lump while he 'does' me?"*

That's it. Just lie there and tune in to your feelings.

"But what am I supposed to feel?"

You are supposed to feel what you feel, no more, no less. No prescriptions. You may feel sexually aroused and if so, fine, just feel it. Don't think for a moment that you have to go anywhere with that feeling or do anything about it. And you may very well feel sexually numb these first few times. Fine. That's perfectly normal. Just feel what you feel and observe it. Don't fall into the trap of thinking, "I should be feeling turned on about now."

You may feel uncomfortable, itchy, ticklish, giddy. Or you may feel so drowsy that you start drifting off to sleep. That's fine, too. (And by the way, Toucher, if your partner does fall asleep while you are touching her, don't take it as rejection. All that means is that she is comfortable and relaxed.)

You may even feel sad. Many men and women find themselves crying during these sessions. Don't push the feeling away. And don't hang on to it when you feel it leaving. Let this emotion flow through you like any of the others.

The fact is, these exercises can elicit any number of unexpected feelings. You may feel tense one moment and then suddenly so relaxed you feel like you are floating. Don't try to control or predict your emotions. Let them surprise you.

"But what if I feel anxious?"

Ah, then you'd be like most everybody else. Many people become anxious the first time they try the Sensual Exercises because they feel foolish, like a kid sent back to first grade. It taps into their general fear of regressing. Others become anxious because they've loaded the first exercise with unrealistic expectations: they want it to solve all the problems in their relationship immediately—in one fell swoop—and when it doesn't, they are sure that their problems are terminal. But probably the major reason Touchees become anxious that first time is that they are worried that their partner, the Toucher, is not enjoying his "job." They are so fixated on what their partner is feeling—or rather, what they think he is feeling—that all they can feel themselves is anxiety. But whatever the reason for the anxiety, the best way to get beyond it is to gently turn your focus to the sensations your body is feeling. Just try to stay with that. All those anxiety-producing ideas are only in your head. And the only purpose they serve is to help you avoid feeling pleasure.

"I don't get it, Dagmar (the Touchee says). *You keep telling me not to pay any attention to my partner, but you just told him that I'm going to be his guide. Which is it?"*

You are his guide, all right, but you are only concerned with what he does to you, not how he feels about it.

All the while that you are the Touchee, you have the right *and* the responsibility to monitor how your partner touches you. You must communicate exactly what you want: where you want to be touched, how hard, how soft, how fast, how slow, and for how long. You correct any touch that is not precisely what you want. And you must communicate all of this nonverbally. That usually means putting your hand over his and literally guiding him and demonstrating for him your heart's—and body's—desires.

"Wouldn't it be a little more civilized, and less aggressive, to communicate this with a gentle word or two?"

No. Words have a way of getting out of hand, of turning a simple instruction into a litany of complaints. "Gentler on my belly" quickly escalates to "Can't you ever do anything gently?" And in no time at all you are fighting, bringing up past offenses, psychoanalyzing each other, jabbering away—everything but paying attention to your body sensations. Words are in your brain and we want to get you out of your brain and into your feelings.

It will take a little practice, but soon you will develop a shorthand of nonverbal communication, simple touches and gestures with which you will cue each other to where you'd like to be touched and how. For most couples, this means lifting the Toucher's hand and moving it to the spot where you want it, pressing down on his hand when you desire more pressure, lifting it up when you desire less pressure, guiding his hand for angle and speed until he is doing exactly what you want. This is a "language" that can never develop into a debate or a forum of recriminations.

Here's how it works: this direct, nonverbal communication frees both of you from the very possibility of guilt and recrimination. The Toucher has no anxiety about touching you "wrong" because he knows that you will correct him if you are not perfectly pleased. He does not have to worry about making mistakes or being inadequate, and he does not have to constantly second-guess your desires. You will be amazed at how liberating this feels. What's more, this allows the Toucher to be more adventurous and creative. He can try "moves" he's never risked before because he knows that if you don't like it, you will simply let him know.

And the Touchee is liberated, too. You don't have to grin and bear touches that are uncomfortable, to deny yourself getting exactly what you want because of some ridiculous bedroom protocol or your fear of appearing too aggressive. The deal you have made with each other gives you permission to ask for and get the pleasure you want.

"Am I supposed to pat him on the head or something when he's touching me just the way I like it?"

No, your only obligation is to make corrections—not to give praise. Once you start "complimenting" your partner on a job well done—say, deliberately moaning and groaning your approval—you are once again diverting your attention from your own feelings. If spontaneous moans escape from your lips, fine, but no production numbers, please. You do not have to encourage the Toucher; you do not have to keep him happy.

"It sounds to me (the Toucher says) *like I'm going to end up feeling like some kind of gigolo, the local hired hand who gives massages on order."*

Terrific. Because now you will finally realize that the only way you are going to get anything out of this for yourself is by focusing on your own sensations. You can either feel like a robot slave or you can feel like a sensualist with the most sensitive fingertips in the world. Ultimately, it's your choice.

"Still, the whole idea of ordering him around just doesn't feel right (the Touchee says). *'Touch me now. Touch me there. Not so hard, faster, slower.' I'll feel like such a selfish pig. And I'll feel so guilty knowing that he's just doing this out of duty."*

Fine, enjoy being a selfish pig. It is probably just what you need to finally get in touch with your own feelings. And, darn it, stop worrying about what *he* is feeling! Let him be in a bad mood if he wants. Let him even be in a rotten, resentful mood. All this insisting that he enjoy every minute of touching you is a sure way of guaranteeing that *neither* of you will have a satisfying experience. The fact is, your preoccupation with how he feels about every activity you do together—not just sex—is ultimately your way of trying to control him. I see more couples go down the tubes because one partner is always saying, "But you don't *really* and *truly* deep down want to go to the movies, do you?" And by the time they sort out all their layers of motives, it's too late to go anywhere. It's maddening. Neither of you ends up knowing what you genuinely feel about anything.

After prescribing these exercises for hundreds of couples, there is one thing I am certain of: your partner is going to feel a whole lot better the moment you stop paying attention to how he feels. Because that's when he finally can be in whatever mood he wants without having to worry about how it affects you! You finally break that stifling cycle of "I-can't-feel-this-way-unless-you-feel-that-way." You can finally stop asking yourself that turn-off question of all time, "Are we having fun yet?"

Yes, these *are* exercises in selfishness. You play out the most fundamental dynamic in your relationship: how to take from each other while leaving each other alone. And you play it out in the bedroom where you've been trained to always think in terms of mutual and simultaneous experiences. We're putting an end to that. Your lovemaking has become corrupted by polite and social behavior, by always looking for responses, by always aiming to please. *But the first step toward heartfelt lovemaking is loving your own sensations.* You become a wonderful lover the moment you become a wonderful taker. Through these exercises you discover that in the end selfishness is the greatest gift you can give to one another—it is the gift of letting your partner be and feel what he wants. And so if he does not seem to be enjoying touching you at this particular moment, you neither have to feel guilty nor grateful. You can just feel the pleasures of his touch.

"Wonderful, Dagmar! So selfishness is the road to happiness. It sounds like the Yuppie credo. But I thought you promised us the road to intimacy, *and that's in the opposite direction from selfishness."*

No, it's actually in the same direction. To achieve genuine intimacy with one another, you must first detach from one another. You must first experience and respect your separateness. You must first acknowledge that your feelings are separate from his, that they are not controlled by either his desires or his moods. Only then can you let go of your emotions, let them flow between you. This is not a paradox, it is a process. Most of us remain isolated in our relationships because we are terrified of drowning in intimacy. *But by becoming selfish, you can dare to be intimate.* By turning off all emotional contact with your partner, you can begin to learn to truly love him. Because only then will you be sure that you will not lose yourself in love and in making love.

"You make it sound so darned impersonal, like we're going to learn how to make it with a tree stump."

No, I just want you to learn how to stop your negative interactions, so you can start making love all over again in a positive way.

But now you've got me doing exactly what I resolved not to do: arguing in the abstract about something you have to experience for yourself. And that is ultimately what these exercises are all about: experiencing the process that takes you through detachment to intimacy. It is a lesson that your body can teach your mind and heart.

So enough talk. Close this book and do not open it for a week. And remember, the experiment begins the moment you say, "I want to be touched now."

 *Chapter 11*

Different Strokes
for Different Folks

End of Week One

I can usually tell the minute a couple walks into my office at the end of the week just how much they have gotten out of the first round of exercises. Some couples stroll in hand-in-hand like adolescent lovebirds—a sure sign that it's starting to work. Other couples arrive with a pronounced chip on their shoulders—usually indicating that they have avoided doing the exercises. And then there are the couples who are already fighting before they even sit down—usually signaling that the exercises have brought to the surface a problem that has been festering between them for years. Responses vary radically, especially this early in the program, but hardly ever is there no response at all. Just confronting the idea of doing these exercises gets emotions going.

You will have to pick your own responses from those that follow: I do not think you should have any difficulty recognizing where you fit. But do yourself and your partner a favor: do not use this chapter as an excuse for going back to "discussing your relationship." That is exactly what we are trying to avoid. Just use the following exchanges to make your next Sensual Exercise more satisfying.

"WE NEVER GOT AROUND TO DOING THE EXERCISES."

Why not?

"We were too busy with our work . . . The children were a problem . . . We had unexpected visitors . . . We had expected visitors . . . We were hardly ever at home at the same time . . . etc., etc." (Pick one.)

All no-time-in-our-schedule excuses are unacceptable. If you do not have time for these exercises, then you do not have time for making love. End of discussion.

If you were in my office, I would remind you that you have wasted another week's fee on nothing at all. What we talk about in my office—or in this book—is of no value to you unless you do the exercises. Just do them and stop being such a baby about it.

"But neither of us was in the mood for it all week."

You don't need to be in the right mood to start the exercises. In fact, waiting for the right mood to descend upon you is one way to end up with no love life at all. Let the exercises affect your mood, not vice versa.

"But I could tell I wasn't going to get anything out of the exercises considering the mood I was in."

Surprise yourself.

"Listen, it couldn't be helped—I just needed the time for sleep."

No, you didn't. Minute for minute, these exercises replace sleeping time. They are that regenerative.

"HEY, WE TRIED. IN FACT, WE WERE JUST ABOUT TO DO THE EXERCISES WHEN WE SUDDENLY GOT INTO THIS HORRENDOUS FIGHT."

Ah yes. By coincidence, of course. Couples frequently have fights before they start their very first exercise—just as some couples routinely get into fights just as they are about to make

159

love. It's anxiety, pure and simple. The "subject" of your fight may be sex or it may be who takes out the garbage, but the effect is the same: it allows you to avoid dealing with the emotions that would be elicited by sensual intimacy. It is a fairly common reaction. Don't worry about it. But next time, go ahead with the exercises anyhow. Remember, you don't have to feel good about one another to start. You just have to start.

"I don't buy that. Listen, I've been royally pissed at him all week because of something truly awful he said. Now I don't know about you, Dagmar, but the idea of allowing myself to be caressed by somebody I'm furious at is just too much for me."

It's not easy, I know. But consider why you cannot allow yourself to be touched by your partner when you are angry at him. Basically, you are probably afraid that you will actually enjoy the sensations, that you will "give in" to the pleasure it affords you and that you will end up feeling good about your partner—and that then you will feel like he "won."

But that really need not be the case. You can enjoy the pleasure of your partner's touch without experiencing it as his victory and your vulnerability. In fact, if you completely focus on your own pleasure, you can experience the exercise as your own victory. After all, you are the one who is making the demand. You are getting what you want from him. You are even allowed to be somewhat vindictive in your timing. For example, wait until he has settled down in front of the Mets game and say "Now. I want to be touched now." You will not feel like a loser that way.

For most couples, the first weeks of this program are exercises in what we call "detaching with love." You learn how to stop focusing on and catering to your partner's desires, while at the same time allowing your loving feelings toward him to grow and flow. But for some of you, your warehouse of anger toward your partner is so large that you must go through a stage of "detaching with anger" before you can begin detaching with love. As your partner starts to touch you, you must say to yourself, "I'm going to enjoy this in spite of my fury at him. No matter how good his caresses feel, he's not going to control me with them. I'm not going to feel grateful or weak. And when we get out of bed, I'm going to be furious at him."

"And this is going to lead to intimacy?"

Indeed it is. Because ultimately the more selfish you get—the more pleasure you allow yourself to take from your partner—the less angry and unsatisfied with your partner you will be. And that is how intimacy starts to grow. All this anger you feel toward your partner has not *replaced* your positive feelings toward him; rather, it has *buried* those positive feelings. This is the first stage in digging those loving feelings out.

"But I'm not just angry at him—I am seriously pissed. If I had a choice, I'd rather slug him than touch him."

If it's really that bad, maybe you ought to let off a little steam just before getting in bed for the exercises. Try some of the Esalen techniques, like firing Ping-Pong balls at each other at ten paces. (Some couples I know prefer rolled-up socks.) Let that hatred flow—give it some air. One bottled-up emotion can bottle them all up.

Another format for fighting that I often recommend is the "hand-holding" argument. You actually hold hands while you take turns slinging your gripes at each other—no interruptions, no defenses allowed. This has a wonderful, paradoxical feel to it. You get your anger out, but you are also forced to "hang in" with each other, to listen to your partner's point of view. Wonder of wonders, after all is screamed and done, you are still there for one another. And the prospect of holding hands all the way to the bedroom may feel like the natural next step.

For some of you, the anger runs so deep that even these techniques will not be enough. For you, I have to make an exception to my no-talking-during-the-exercises rule. During the first few sessions, express your anger *out loud* while you are touching or being touched. Let yourself experience the paradox of saying, "I really can't stand you," while you are feeling the pleasure of his touch. In time, you will find your anger running out of steam as you gradually focus more and more on your sensations.

"But what about me? (the Toucher asks). How am I supposed to keep caressing her while listening to her go on about how she can't stand me?"

You don't have to listen to her. Just do your job—your homework. You can even pretend you are polishing a table. You are detaching now. Don't worry about how "the table" feels about you.

"I WAS WILLING TO DO THE EXERCISES, BUT SHE WAS THE FIRST TOUCHER AND SHE NEVER INITIATED."

Don't get into a self-righteous argument about it. But starting right now, switch. *You* are now the first Toucher. Make it happen.

"WE DID THE EXERCISES, BUT WHAT A BORE IT WAS. I DIDN'T FEEL A THING."

Nothing at all?

"Well, not much. Maybe a little tingle for the first few minutes, but after that it all sort of blanded out."

Could it be that that "tingle" made you anxious? That you got a little hint of the torrent of feelings that could start flowing if you let them, so you clamped down, put a lid on the whole experience, and decided that you had "blanded out?"

"No way. I simply didn't feel very much. Except when it started to tickle and then I knew I'd had enough."

But ticklishness is a sure sign of nervousness—or at the very least, giddiness. If it were simply a physical reflex, you would be able to tickle yourself—and you can't. I think we had better get clear right now on the fact that *you are in control of your sensations.* When you feel nothing but numbness (or tickles) while your partner touches you, that is because *you* have turned yourself off to feeling anything more.

Prove it to yourself right now.

Caress the inside of your left forearm with the fingertips of your right hand. Relax, push away all anxious thoughts, close your eyes, and focus on the sensations you feel.

Now, caress yourself in the same way while focusing on your anxieties. Think about what a pain in the neck these exercises are: consider all the better things you could (and should) be doing now; concentrate on the noises you hear in the next room.

Now, examine the difference between the two caresses—or rather the difference between the way you experienced each of them. Undoubtedly, the first caress gave you more pleasure.

It is a simple point, but one we always need to be reminded of: when we feel "nothing," it is because we are letting nothing in.

"Okay, I felt a little something, but nothing worth writing home about."

You mean, you didn't feel sexually aroused?

"Right."

And feeling anything less than sexually aroused means you hardly feel anything at all, right? Where do you get the idea that every time a hand is laid on your naked body you should instantly become charged with sexual feelings? That expectation not only guarantees that these exercises will be a failure, but that *you* will feel like a failure too. You think, "Ten minutes and I still don't have an erection," and that anxiety gets translated into the defense of, "I feel numb and bored and want to stop this nonsense."

But there are a host of deep, sensual feelings available to us that do not immediately shoot to our genitals and prepare us for sex. And once you are comfortable with that fact and stop "waiting" for your sexual responses, you can start to experience the difference between doing sex and making love. By allowing yourself to linger with sensuality, you are going to start loving each little step of lovemaking. You are going to become a connoisseur of your own feelings.

🐌

"BUT HE TOUCHES ME THE SAME WAY HE MAKES LOVE— LIKE A CLUNK. HE'S SIMPLY INCAPABLE OF CARESSING ME IN A SENSUAL WAY."

What did he do wrong?

"His hands are too rough . . . His hands are too cold . . . He pats me like I'm dog . . . He always goes back to the same spot . . . He's totally unimaginative in the way he does it, totally uninspired . . . etc., etc." (Pick as many as you like.)

You sound to me as if you focused on everything you disliked about the experience and nothing that you liked about it, so of course there was nothing to enjoy.

But more to the point, you apparently have not guided your Toucher well—and that is your responsibility. If he touches you too roughly, show him exactly how you want to be touched. If his hands are cold, warm them for him. The jig is up. You can't blame him for not "doing you right" anymore.

"But he's such a slow learner. When it was my turn to be Toucher, I touched him exactly the way I like to be touched. You'd think he'd get the hint."

But how (and how long) you touch your partner does not have a thing to do with how he does or should touch you. They are totally separate experiences, not lessons you are giving one another. You are different people with different desires and different sensibilities. It takes different strokes for different folks. And love is recognizing that you don't feel the same thing in the place or at the same time.

"I'll tell you what gets me really angry though. A few minutes after he finished fondling me like he had lead weights on his wrists, I saw him pick up the cat and pet it ever so delicately. I actually envied that cat."

Great. Now you know he is capable of touching you just the way you want. All you have to do is communicate that to him.

"Okay, but when he is the Toucher and I move his hand, he just stays where I put it until I move it again. And as if that's not bad enough, I catch him yawning all the time. Come on, how am I supposed to get carried away with all these powerful emotions you talk about when I'm being fondled by a bored, uninspired lover? Is that my fault, too?"

Give him a chance to change, would you? It takes time to develop a nonverbal language that will quickly communicate to him what you want. It will also take time for him to relax enough to respond to your desires. Those yawns of his are not really yawns of boredom, they are yawns of anxiety. You have probably let him know more than once that you find him a clumsy lover, so he undoubtedly felt like a failure before he even began the exercise. It is not easy to be a responsive lover (or Toucher) when it feels like a test.

My guess is that you have this dream of an expert lover who knows exactly where and when and how you want to be touched before you yourself do. But that is just the kind of dream that prevents you from ever experiencing sensations in the here and now. Believe me, you are the only expert on your own desires.

I'll say it one more time. Just focus on your own sensations, not on what you think your partner feels about touching you.

"LOOK, I'VE TRIED GUIDING HIM AND GIVING HIM COR-RECTIONS WHEN HE TOUCHES ME, BUT HE GETS SO DEFEN-SIVE THAT I FINALLY HAD TO GIVE UP AND JUST SUFFER WHAT HE GAVE ME."

How could you tell he was defensive?

"When I moved his hand for the tenth time he shouted, 'You're never satisfied with anything I do! There's no use even trying to please you! You're just impossible!'"

That does sound a wee bit defensive, doesn't it?

"That's not defensive, it's the truth! (her partner interjects). *She's never satisfied. I mean, I don't complain and correct all the time when she touches me.*

165

I'm not saying I like everything she did to me, but I'm not going to be a spoiled sport about it."

No martyrdom, please. You still don't seem to understand that these corrections are not personal criticisms, they are simple communications. They are actually a way of freeing your partner from the worry of touching you in a way that you do not like.

But there is only one way I can break you out of this cycle you've gotten yourselves into. For the next week, *you* (the defensive partner) must make a minimum of *five* corrections whenever you are the Touchee. And *you* (the critical partner) cannot make *more than five* corrections when you are Touchee. Now, perhaps you can stop competing with and criticizing each other and get back to your sensations.

"I CAN'T BELIEVE THE WAY HE WANTS ME TO TOUCH HIM. HE WANTS ME TO KNEAD HIS BACK AND MASSAGE HIS CALVES LIKE I'M HIS GYM TRAINER, NOT HIS LOVER. IT'S JUST AS I THOUGHT: THE MAN DOESN'T HAVE A SENSUAL FEELING IN HIS BODY."

For once in your life, give your partner what he wants instead of what you think he should want. That is the ultimate gift. That is the respect that leads to genuine intimacy.

"SHE PICKED THE EXACT WORST TIME TO SAY 'I WANT TO BE TOUCHED NOW.' I WAS RIGHT IN THE MIDDLE OF WATCHING THE BALL GAME."

That's probably why she picked that time—because she was sick and tired of seeing you always getting involved in something other than her.

"But that's hardly a way to get me in the right mood for this stuff."

Don't be so precious about your moods. She got your attention, didn't she?

"HE PICKED THE EXACT WORST TIME TO SAY 'I WANT TO BE TOUCHED NOW.' HE WAITED UNTIL ELEVEN-THIRTY AND I COULD BARELY KEEP MY EYES OPEN."

He probably had been thinking about it all evening and he was so anxious that he kept putting it off. No doubt it's very difficult for him to ask for pleasure this way. Don't hold it against him.

"WHEN IT'S HIS TURN TO BE TOUCHED, HE ALWAYS KEEPS HIS EYE ON THE CLOCK AND STOPS AS SOON AS THE FIFTEEN-MINUTE MINIMUM IS UP. BUT WHEN IT'S MY TURN, I FEEL LIKE TAKING A LOT LONGER THAN THAT. YET I FEEL TOO GUILTY TO TAKE IT."

Don't feel guilty, just feel lucky. Lucky that you are capable of getting more out of this. Take your full forty-five minutes, if that's what you feel like. Maybe it will help your partner take longer for himself next time around.

But as for *you* (the Touchee who can never take more than the fifteen-minute minimum), I want you to add five minutes to each session starting with the next one—right up until you can finally take your eyes off the clock. You are probably still intimidated about being passive, still uptight about allowing yourself to "selfishly" take in pleasure. All I tell you is, "Try it, you'll like it." You will not lose all your strength or fall apart or turn into a wimp. On the contrary. You will become stronger and more alive.

"WE CHEATED. AFTER ABOUT TEN MINUTES OF STROKING HER BELLY, I COULDN'T RESIST ANY LONGER AND WENT FOR HER BREASTS. (OR VAGINA) (OR BOTH) BUT IT WAS FABU-

LOUS. WE WERE BOTH MORE TURNED ON THAN WE'VE BEEN IN YEARS."

Congratulations. But you have managed to miss the whole point of the program. You are still so preoccupied with *doing* sex that you continue to deprive yourself of the joys of lingering with sensuality, of floating with pointless pleasure.

"*But you don't understand, Dagmar. Our sex life has been pretty tepid for years. This turn-on was a rare opportunity. We didn't want to let it get away.*"

Don't get me wrong; I am glad you were more turned on than you have been in a very long time. And let me reassure you, this is just the beginning of a series of sensual surprises that these exercises have in store for you. In short, you'll be turned on that way again and again—it is not going to go away. That is, unless you persist in short-circuiting the rest of your feelings. But what you have done is to *cut off a whole gamut of other feelings by diving for sex.* If you stick with the program, you can have it all: strong, intimate feelings *and* powerful sex.

"*WE CHEATED AND MADE LOVE. YOU TOLD US TO GET LOST IN OUR FEELINGS, RIGHT? WELL, OUR FEELINGS LED STRAIGHT TO SEX.*"

Listen, arousal comes and goes. Get used to that fact and then you can depend on it. You won't have to seize every opportunity as if it were the last.

"*That's not what I'm talking about, Dagmar. We just got to that point where it would have been too painful to stop. I spent my whole adolescence being sexually frustrated—I see no reason to subject myself to that kind of torture now.*"

Ah yes, the famous "blue balls" defense. Well, if you really find it that uncomfortable not to "finish off," you always have the option to masturbate once the session is over.

"*Are you kidding? Right then and there?*"

Or you can retire to another room if you're feeling shy about it.

"Now you've gone too far, Dagmar. You're really trying to freak us out, aren't you?"

Not freak you out, just loosen you up. But we don't have to get into that "ultimate secret" now, if you don't want to. It will keep for later.

"SOMETHING FABULOUS HAPPENED LAST WEEK. THE FIRST TWO SESSIONS NOTHING MUCH HAPPENED. IN FACT, WE WERE THINKING OF GIVING UP ON THE WHOLE BUSINESS. BUT DURING THAT THIRD SESSION, I STARTED TO FEEL SO MUCH THAT I ACTUALLY STARTED TO CRY. I FELT SO SAFE AND LOVED AND EXCITED AND ALIVE ALL AT ONCE. AND I FELT THIS IMMENSE GRATITUDE TOWARD MY PARTNER WELLING UP INSIDE ME, GRATITUDE FOR THE PLEASURE HE WAS GIVING ME. BUT FOR ONCE, THAT GRATITUDE WASN'T TINGED WITH GUILT OR FEAR OF BEING OVERWHELMED BY HIM. IT WAS PURE AND I COULD FEEL MY LOVE FOR HIM FLOWING THROUGH ME."

"It was special for me too (her partner says). *It was just so liberating to forget being a 'good lover' for once and to get into my own sensations. It was like my whole body was crawling out of a cocoon. And the irony is, I've never pleased her more, nor have I ever felt more sexual."*

Wonderful. You're ready to move on to the next stage.

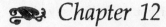 *Chapter 12*

Making a Mess of
Your Love Life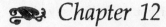

Week Two

I remember a friend of mine who went to Paris to study painting. For the first half year his teacher only permitted him to put one pigment plus white on his palette.

"I learned an incredible amount about seeing and creating in those six months," he told me later. "I could never have imagined all the effects I could create just using green."

For the next week I want you to see how many "effects" you can create—how sensual you can get and how many taboos you can break—while *still* not touching breasts or genitals. The format remains the same: you again take turns initiating three double sessions during the course of the week. But now it's time to get more creative. I want you to explore all the different ways you can touch one another and all the different places where you can do it.

Caress your partner's back with your feet. Stroke his belly with your hair. Explore her navel with your tongue. Run your fingernails along the insides of his thighs. Rub your cheek against her buttocks. The combinations are endless and endlessly delicious. Anything is possible. *Unless, of course, it makes your partner uncomfortable: the Touchee always retains veto power; she can always make corrections.*

Remember the delight of a sweet breath in your ear? Followed by the flick of a tongue? Of sucking on the skin of your lover's neck? For too many of us, these pleasures have been sacrificed to pure and efficient genital sex. Let's bring these pleasures back. Linger with them.

Now is the time to break out of the goal-oriented routine of always relating your naked bodies to one another for maximum stimulation of your genitals. Think of all you have been missing: your poor, neglected (and often very sensual) feet; your affection-starved back; your yearning neck.

Stretch your imagination. Pull props from your closet, from the bathroom cabinet, from the refrigerator, from your child's toy shelf. Tease a feather up and down her legs. Shake your fur coat across his back. Rub baby oil all over his feet. Dab a powder puff in circles around her buttocks. Spread fingerpaints across his belly and paint him a picture of a cat. Search for new sensations that you can give and that you want to receive.

And search for new places to try them out. Switch venues and you break tired routines and habitual responses. For once, get out of the bedroom; it reeks with routines and expectations. Take her into the living room, spread a comforter on the floor and then spread her on top of it. Start a session in the shower—with sponge and soap. Set him on top of the dining room table. And while you are at it, have a banquet off his body. Spread jam on his loins and lick him clean. Fill his navel with maple syrup and drink deep. Feast on whipped cream from his chest and belly.

Get loose, get playful, and above all, get messy.

It is virtually impossible to abandon yourself to a full range of sensual feelings if you are preoccupied with keeping clean. Gently push yourself across those borders of purity and order; tap into that delicious childhood realm of mud pies and playing with your food. Allowing yourself these small, harmless transgressions can release volumes of feeling. By permitting yourself to get a little messy with jam or whipped cream, a little daring with furs or feathers, deep-seated sexual inhibitions become unmoored from the ever-present idea that our bodies are dirty and distasteful. And in the process of "making a mess of your love life," you discover that, lo and behold, your life does not fall apart, you do not lose all self-control, and you do not become stricken with disease.

What I really want you to do is to bring sensuality into *all* of your life. Sensuality has a wonderful way of trickling from one part of your life to another. I have always maintained that if you learned how to eat sensually—to chew languorously, to run your tongue around the inside of your mouth, to smack your lips, to savor the texture of each morsel and the subtleties of each spice —you would automatically begin to make love more sensuously. And vice versa.

As couples move into this stage of the Sensual Exercises, they report all kinds of new sensations entering their lives.

"People at the office tell me I've turned into some kind of hedonist," one woman told me with unabashed pride. "I'm always brushing a silk scarf against my cheek or slipping my fingers inside my blouse and idly stroking my belly. I've become a regular Sybarite."

Another woman told me that she suddenly switched from being a shower person to taking long hot baths every evening simply because it felt so good. She even reported that she had discovered something sensual about washing the dishes in warm, soapy water.

Similarly, a husband told me that he suddenly found himself enjoying taking the dog out for a walk "because the evening air feels so good against my skin."

These people were experiencing a renaissance of their own sensuality.

"I feel like I'm coming out of an anesthetic," one woman told me. "I didn't realize how numb I'd been until I started the exercises."

Most significantly, couples soon begin to see changes in the way they relate to each other and that, too, begins at the sensual level. They find themselves touching each other during the course of the day in ways that had been lost to them for years.

"We have a small kitchen and we used to be forever dodging each other in it," a woman named Evelyn told me. "But after we really got into the exercises, we just let ourselves bump into each other. Friendly bumps and do-si-dos. Even a few old-time snuggles. I don't know what's going on, but I like it."

For years, Evelyn had only experienced sex with her husband as her "wifely obligation." Not only were the Sensual Exercises resensitizing her to the pleasures of touch, but they were releasing both her and her husband from the idea that every touch had to be a prelude to genital sex. This was "no strings" touching, no "follow-through" required, so she was free to enjoy "bumps and do-si-dos" in themselves. The paradox, of course, was that this prepared her to finally take her own pleasure in sex later on in the program.

But it does not stop there. Relaxed sensual contact opens the door to a more loving relationship. It is really quite simple: when you give each other pleasure, you start to like each other more. As you get into the exercises you may very well find yourselves fighting less, particularly about petty matters.

"It's not like the issues have changed," a husband who had been fighting with his wife for years told me. "I mean, we still have all the same old differences, but I just can't seem to get as worked up about them as I used to."

"You just took all the fun out of our fights," his wife chimed in with mock anger. "Now we'd rather do something dull like hold hands and have a pleasant conversation. We're turning into such a banal couple."

After a few weeks of the exercises, couples frequently tell me that they find talking to each other much more satisfying. I think this is largely because the exercises allow us to concretely experience each other's separateness. We learn that when she feels one thing and he feels another, that does not mean that their relationship is falling apart. It just means that they are separate people with separate sensibilities. And so in conversation, too, we discover that we can calmly listen to each other's differences— our different experiences and different points of view—without seeing them as a threat; we know we won't lose ourselves.

But by far the best early "fallout" of the Sensual Exercises was described to me by a thirty-year-old woman with a twinkle in her eye.

"I actually *blushed* like a teenager when Carl [her husband] met me at my office the other day," she said. "I was just happy to see him, simple as that. Can you imagine?"

I can indeed. This happy young woman was once again perceiving her husband as a source of pleasure and comfort. Her body had recently relearned that and now the message had gone out to her mind and heart and, apparently, her glowing cheeks.

"This is all very nice except for one thing, Dagmar: I've got the nagging feeling that I'm trading in sex for some kind of neutered, lovey-dovey affection. How long can we forgo real sex before we end up relating to each other like eunuchs?"

Don't worry. You are in the process of getting more turned on to each other, not less. But for once you are not simply limiting yourself to erotic/genital feelings. The sex is still there; it won't go away. You simply are not going to do anything about it. Not yet.

🦑

But now I want you to add an element to your sessions that will make the difference between doing sex and making love even clearer to you. I am talking about *kissing*.

I am perpetually amazed by how many couples come to me

who are doing sex regularly, often including oral-genital sex, yet who have virtually abandoned sensual, lip-to-lip kissing. Some only kiss during sexual intercourse; others even avoid it then. No, for them kissing has been reduced to quick, anemic pecks, more of a salute than an intimate sensual contact.

And there is a reason for that. In its way, kissing is a far more intimate act than sexual intercourse. Face to face, we cannot deny each other's individuality. When we kiss, we cannot depersonalize the experience or lose ourselves in a fantasy about another person. All of that is far easier to do if we are merely grinding our sex organs together. I have the feeling that ever since the Sexual Revolution, when sex became more casual and hence less personal, kissing has become even more emotionally loaded. This thought occurred to me when I talked with a call girl who told me that the one act she will not perform for her clients is kissing; that is reserved for her lover only. That is her last intimacy.

But along with intimacy comes anxiety. For many people deep, sensual kisses activate childhood fears of being "swallowed up" by Mommy. Somewhere deep in our marrow we remember the helplessness we felt when we submitted to Mother's wet smackers and some of us still feel that helplessness when we "submit" to our partner's kisses. The wetness in itself can be anxiety-producing for many people. Again, it feels too messy, too primal. Somehow, we can deal with the wetness of our genitals—they are "down there." But up here, we might drown in it.

During the next week, we are going to start your kissing life all over again. In the middle of each session—when you are switching roles from Touchee to Toucher—I want you to experiment with kissing. As with the rest of these exercises, you must alternate between being the active and the passive partner. And as always, the passive partner is in complete control. If for any reason the kissing becomes too much for you, too anxiety-making, you can pull away or slow things down.

At the beginning, you are both permitted to keep your eyes

closed—we're going to let intimacy in gradually. And also at the beginning, see if you can keep your bodies from touching—we are going to focus all your sensations on your lips, tongue, and mouth. Again, go slowly and concentrate on the sensations you feel. Do not attend to how and if your partner is responding; that is irrelevant for now. Brush your lips against hers. Feel their softness, their "bounce." Trace your tongue around her lips, the outline, then the part between them. Slowly press your lips to hers. Suck and tug at them. Slowly slide your tongue inside her mouth. Feel the warmth and wetness. Withdraw the moment either of you feels uncomfortable or "invaded."

This first time, limit yourselves to five minutes apiece. But next time, go twice as long if you both want to. Also next time, the "passive" kisser may kiss back if he wants to—but he is under no obligation to. And this time you may both begin the exercise with your eyes open and then close them.

Eye contact, like kissing, is fraught with anxieties about intimacy. Our eyes, we are told, are the windows of our souls and we are warned that people who avoid eye contact—who look down or away when we search their faces—are avoiding intimacy, hiding their souls. Many of the New Age therapies spawned in the sixties that put a high premium on openness and intimacy, made eye contact exercises central to group and couple therapy. But I believe that any forcing of eye contact runs the risk of taking us further away from intimacy, not closer to it. It can become a form of intimidation, even bullying, of playing subtle power games of "More Open and Soulful than Thou." Such exercises too easily turn into that childhood contest of "Staring Until You Laugh" where you actually have to turn off your feelings in order to win. In an adult relationship, the obligation to look at one another may distract us from other feelings, too, particular sensual feelings, so I am loathe to prescribe it as a necessary stop toward intimacy. Yet on the other hand, it *is* true that when we are capable of looking openly and undefensively into one another's eyes, marvelous feelings can flow between us, incredible connections can be made. So I do want you to experiment with eye contact, but *while always remaining in full control of the experience.*

Start "sneaking" looks at your partner during this second kissing session. Do not force feelings—do not try to "beam" messages of love through your eyes. And do not wait for powerful feelings to be stirred inside you. The moment *either* of you feels the least bit uncomfortable or "invaded," close your eyes. No blame and no recriminations allowed. As with all the rest of this program, we are making intimate contact with one another very gradually. We have to be comfortable with each step before we go on to the next.

Now we come to the real old-time homework aspect of this second week of the program. I want you each to keep a personal notebook, a Sensual Diary, on your side of your bed—preferably in a private drawer of the bed table. And immediately after each double session, I want you each to take out your notebook and record in detail the experiences you have just had by responding in detail to each question of my questionnaire.

"Good grief, Dagmar, just when these exercises were finally starting to sound like fun, you turn it into a research project. One minute you tell us to get out of our heads and into our feelings, and the next you tell us we have to become self-conscious little diarists. Which is it?"

Both. Responding to the questionnaire will force you to pay closer attention to your sensations. As a result, next session you will be more attuned to different shadings of feelings and to the various ways you stop yourself from feeling. In the short run, keeping the notebook may make you self-conscious, but ultimately it will lead you to feeling more.

QUESTIONNAIRE

1. Who initiated the session and when?

   a. If it was you, how did it feel to initiate? Give as detailed a response as possible. Did you have to overcome a great deal of shyness or fear of rejection?

b. Once you had initiated, how did you feel about yourself? Proud? Ashamed? Giddy?

2. Did you initiate the session outside the bedroom?

a. If not, what do you think inhibited you from trying a new location?

b. If so, how did it make you feel? Adventurous? Frightened? Giddy? Turned on?

3. Which did you like better, being the Toucher or the Touchee?

4. Did being the Touchee make you nervous?

a. Did it make you feel guilty to selfishly focus only on your own pleasure? Or did the idea that you and your partner are taking turns makes it easier for you to guiltlessly accept the pleasure?

b. (Men) Did it make you feel weak and emasculated to lie there passively while your partner caressed you? Or could you get into being fussed over, as if by a masseur or a geisha?

c. Was it difficult for you to resist touching back?

5. Could you ever completely forget about your partner and become totally absorbed in your own sensations?

6. Did you worry about whether or not you were turned on sexually?

a. (Men) Did you check to see if you had an erection? (Women) Did you check to see if you were lubricating? Or were you able to forget about your genitals and just focus on the sensations you were feeling?

b. Did you find the exercises sexually frustrating or could you linger with arousal without becoming obsessed with having an orgasm?

7. Where did you enjoy being touched the most? Be as specific as you can.

   a. Did you discover a part of your body that felt good to be touched?

   b. Draw a map of your body and shade in the parts (front and back) that were most sensitive and responsive.

8. What kinds of touches gave you the more pleasure?

   a. Describe the sensation. Be as detailed and poetic as you possibly can.

9. Did the touches make you feel emotional? Excited? Tranquil? Sexually turned on? Dreamy? Elated? Loving? Soulful? Melancholy?

10. How did your feelings change over the course of the session?

11. How many times did you "steer" and "correct" your partner's touches?

   a. Did you feel like correcting more, but were afraid of hurting your partner's feelings or seeming too demanding?

   b. Was there anything your partner did which inhibited you from correcting more?

12. What made you decide to move your partner's hand from one part of your body to another? Did one spot feel like it had had enough? Or did another spot "yearn" for some attention?

13. How long did you allow yourself to be touched?

   a. What was the reason you decided to end the session?

Did you really want to take longer but felt that that would make you too much of a "pig"?
b. Do you think you can take more time next session?

14. Did you find it boring to be the Toucher?
a. Did you keep hoping that your partner would tell you that she/he had had enough?

15. Were you worried that you were not doing a good job?
a. Did you feel angry, defensive, or hurt when your partner made corrections? Why do you think it made you feel that way?

16. Were you ever able to take pleasure for yourself in touching your partner or were you too involved in how your partner was responding to feel anything of your own?

17. Does it feel like anything has changed for you as a result of the session? Did any new feelings come up?

18. Did you learn anything about yourself that you did not know before?

Responding to this questionnaire is an opportunity to be perfectly honest with yourself. Resist the temptation to simply say "It felt great" and leave it at that. Push yourself to record the smallest details of your experience. Write down (for example), "At first I was feeling hesitant and guilty about asking him to touch me and for the first few minutes I got lost in wondering how he felt about it instead of focusing on my own feelings. . . ." Believe me, when you can tune in to subtle differences and fluctuations of your feelings, you are on the road to becoming much more sensual than if you simply feel "great" all the time.

And now comes the really hard part. At the end of this second week of the program, I want the two of you to make a date to read your diaries to each other. Pick a spot outside your home, say in a coffee shop or bar. There, one at a time, read your entries out loud to each other.

"You've got to be kidding, Dagmar. You're determined to humiliate us in front of each other, aren't you?"

Quite to the contrary. You aren't going to feel humiliated; you're going to feel relieved. This is going to be one of the most liberating experiences you've ever had because you are finally going to have the opportunity to acknowledge that you have *separate experiences.* And what a relief it is to be free of that absurd notion that you always feel the same thing at the same time.

"But this 'confession' is going to take the last bit of romance out of our relationship. It's going to turn the whole thing into group therapy."

No, it won't. Because the rules are: no discussion, no criticisms, and no analysis allowed. While you read your entry from your Sensual Diary, your partner is only permitted to listen. He cannot interrupt, grimace, or even roll his eyes in disbelief. And after you are done, he is definitely not allowed to criticize or analyze your report.

Heaven knows, he will be tempted to. Most people are positive that their partner has "made a mistake" or "gotten it all wrong." They simply cannot believe that their partner had a different experience from the one they had. One man I worked with, Bill, was convinced that his wife, Ruth, was always lying in her diary.

"She wrote down that I squeezed her calves, but I know I didn't—I just patted them. She even got the temperature of the room wrong—she said it was cool and it was really quite warm."

"But you didn't have the same experience!" I told him for about the tenth time. "Your pat is her squeeze. There's no objective truth here. You have to learn how to listen to Ruth without pushing your point of view on her."

Bill, of course, was threatened by the idea that he could not completely control what his wife was feeling. It took him quite a few diary readings before he discovered that this actually relieved him of the *responsibility* for his wife's feelings, that he did not always have to feel guilty when she was not feeling what she wanted to feel.

Some people are tempted to interrupt their partners' readings because their feelings get hurt. When one husband reported that he grew bored touching his wife, she burst out, "Oh God, and I was feeling so good. Now you've ruined it for me."

"But you *did* feel good," I told her. "And nothing he says can take that away from you. Once you truly believe that, you'll both feel a lot better."

The truth is that it is much easier for us to admit that we felt rotten while our partner was having a wonderful time than it is for us to admit that we felt good while our partner was feeling bored. As always, we would rather blame our partner than feel guilty toward him.

Perhaps the most destructive temptation is to psychoanalyze your partner's responses. One wife I know nodded her head all the way through her husband's report and then said, "You've just proved what I've always said—you're a very inhibited person, just like your father."

God deliver us all from spouses who think they are our therapists. It is one of the great scourges of our time. Often done in the name of "openness," it is a sure way to prevent any intimacy in a relationship.

So in short, shut up and respect your partner's individuality. It takes courage to read from your diary, courage and trust. Some couples find it easier to read to each other if they hold hands across the table and I am all for it. After your partner reads his entry from his Sensual Diary, it is your turn to read yours. And then it is time to close your notebooks and order dinner.

 *Chapter 13*

Sharing Your Most
Intimate Secret

Week Three

You have come to that point in the Graduated Sensual Exercises where you are ready to let genital sex back into your life.

But we are going to reintroduce sex in a totally new way. For just this week, I want you to finish off each of your three double sessions by masturbating simultaneously in front of each other—what I call "tandem masturbation." I know this may sound like just the opposite of intimacy, but believe me, once you dare to break through this barrier, once you share your ultimate secret with each other, you have a chance to experience an intimacy so profound that every aspect of your relationship will be enriched by it forever after. This is no idle claim. Time and time again I have seen tandem masturbation become a breakthrough experience for couples. In this one simple act, layers of inhibitions lift away, years of sexual misunderstandings disappear. Suddenly, two people who have never been able to make genuine contact with each other become intimately connected.

"It was like a flash of heightened awareness," Lester told me. "Mystical, I'd say, except it was so absolutely vivid. For the first time in my life I totally saw Margot [his wife] as a sexual person with feelings and fears of her own just like myself. It was like, 'Shazam! she's not just in my head, she's real and I love her!' "

Not everyone experiences their first tandem masturbation quite as dramatically as this man had, but I have grown used to hearing people say that "barriers dropped away" and, especially, that their partner suddenly seemed so "real." Most significantly, after going through this experience most couples begin relating to one another differently—with greater empathy and with considerably less anxiety and anger. And when it comes to making sensual contact with each other, their feelings are much stronger, their sense of intimacy much more intense. It is an act of revelation that works.

"Great, it works—just like shock therapy. But I'd rather get my shocks from electrodes than put myself through this. I refuse to expose and humiliate myself in front of my partner in this way. It just feels ugly and totally unnecessary."

Look, I know the prospect of shared masturbation is frightening. That is precisely why it is so important to make yourself do it—to get beyond that fear. Once you have tried this exercise, you discover that you don't die of shame, nor do you annihilate your partner. And once you actually experience that fact, a huge burden is lifted from your relationship.

"What burden? You act like I've always had this burning desire to do this tandem masturbation thing with my partner. Well, the very idea never entered my wildest fantasies. So doing it isn't going to relieve anything."

Yes it is. Because over the years I have become convinced that your feelings about your own and your partner's masturbation reflect your most fundamental feelings about your own and your partner's sexuality. It tells you what you feel is "dirty" about sex and what you feel is selfish about it, what frightens you about your partner's sexuality and what threatens your own sexuality about it. It is quite remarkable what hidden feelings are revealed when you try this exercise.

Many women have never actually *seen* their husbands ejaculate and just that prospect repels many of them.

"I can very happily go through the rest of my life without having to witness him spill his mess all over the place, thank you," one grimacing wife named Rhoda L. protested. "Let's face it, some things in life are better left unseen."

"You mean it's okay for him to put that mess in your vagina where you don't have to see it," I said to her. "But then what does that make your vagina—a garbage can?"

I thought it was particularly important for Rhoda to see her husband ejaculate. I was positive that the actuality of the experience would be quite benign compared to the way she imagined it. And then she could finally stop seeing sex as ugly and degrading. In fact, when she finally did force herself to watch her husband masturbate to climax, she burst out laughing.

"Max [her husband] was hurt at first," she told me. "He thought I was making fun of him. But then I explained that I was laughing at myself. I mean, I've been married to the guy for twenty years: I've seen him in the bathroom a thousand times; seen him throw up, pass out, and break out in hives. Why had I made such a big deal out of this?"

In one fell swoop, this woman had demystified sex, desensitized herself from some exaggerated notion of sexual "filth" which had inhibited her.

"Demystified? She's reduced sex to the same level as bathroom functions. What ever happened to romance?"

Romance cannot begin until we stop feeling so anxious with each other. For Rhoda to truly love Max's body, she first had to see it as *real.* Yes, this was the same body she saw daily in the bathroom; it was neither dangerous nor dirty. It was a body that gave him pleasure—*and it could do the same for her.*

The husband of another woman reported to me that when they first tried tandem masturbation and he was about to come, his wife suddenly covered her ears. She was afraid he was literally going to explode in front of her eyes. This woman was finally able to start loving her husband's penis when she saw that it was not a firecracker.

Yet there are many men, too, who feel that masturbating in front of their wives demeans their wives.

"Lucy's a very sensitive woman," Arnold told me privately. "I don't want to put her through this."

"You mean, you think she's too sensitive for sex?" I replied.

This was a couple who had been making love less and less frequently over the years, both claiming that they had simply lost the urge. But I was sure that the urge was still there, it had just been buried in their anxieties. And a fundamental anxiety was Arnold's feeling that his wife was "above" the ugliness of carnality. He had put his wife up on a pedestal and himself down in the sewer. No wonder they had lost the urge: in those positions they could never reach each other.

Arnold's attitude was similar to a great many other men's. He saw his own sexuality as dirty and destructive. It could "hurt" a "good woman." For both him and his wife to start taking pleasure from each other, she had to be demystified; she had to be brought down off that pedestal and into bed with him. Well, tandem masturbation got her off that pedestal fast. The exercise proved far easier for her to try than Arnold could have ever imagined.

"God, what a turn on!" Arnold reported after their first tandem session. He had made the remarkable discovery that his wife was as sexual as he was. Far from being "hurt" by seeing him masturbate, she had been relieved and excited to be brought down to earth and into the realm of relaxed and "messy" pleasure. It had given her the courage to fulfill her end of the bargain —to simultaneously masturbate in front of him. The urge had suddenly returned to both of them.

"From that day on, we've been like two different people," Arnold told me several weeks later. "And let me tell you, the best part is we're not so darned *careful* around each other anymore."

Indeed, most relationships are plagued by too much "careful-ness" and it is virtually impossible to feel intimate if you are always being careful. The ultimate gift of tandem masturbation is mutual acceptance. Both partners carry a new consciousness of each other: "I've seen you in your most private moment, in your primal nakedness. And you have seen me in that nakedness, too. We have shared our most private secret and we are still there for each other. And that is about as intimate as two people can get."

"I've got to hand it to you, Dagmar, only you could make masturbation sound like an act of intimacy. But you very conveniently forget one thing: masturbation is something you do alone. You don't need anybody else around to do it."

And that is why the very idea of seeing your partner mastur-bate makes so many people anxious. You confront one of your greatest fears: that she (or he) is better at satisfying herself than you can ever be. Men, in particular, are frequently tortured by this fear: "I could never last that long, be that hard, move that fast. Who could ever manipulate her so knowingly? Who can compete with her own hand?"

Conversely, some people whose partners have grown sexually inattentive resist the very mention of this exercise because it reminds them of all the rejection they've been experiencing.

"Hey, masturbation is just about the sum total of my sex life these days," a middle-aged wife said to me. "All this exercise is going to do is remind me of that—remind me that we haven't made love together in God knows how long."

"Just bring your secret out of the closet for now," I assured her. "You cannot be comfortably attached to your husband un-less you are comfortable with your own sexuality. And that's the first step toward getting your mutual sex life going again."

Many people—particularly women—are upset by the idea of tandem masturbation for the flip side of that reason: because they are afraid of making their partners feel inadequate.

"I know what Henry [her husband] will be thinking," Wendy

told me. "That I'm better at this than he is. No, worse—that he's such a lousy lover I have to do it for myself."

"Take that risk," I told her. "But my guess is that he'll be relieved—if not at first, then later on."

Henry was a man who constantly lived with the fear of being an inadequate lover: a fear that is one of the great self-fulfilling prophecies of all time. The burden of believing that his wife had to go through life feeling sexually frustrated if he didn't do his "job" properly had made Henry retreat from that job altogether. It was a vicious circle, but fortunately the tandem masturbation exercise cut right through it. Rather than dropping more deeply into his sense of inadequacy, Henry was instantly relieved to see that Wendy could satisfy her own sexual needs. It took the pressure off him. Wendy was not dependent on him for orgasms; now they could get together with one another without all the anxieties of a relationship loaded down with dependencies. It allowed Henry to begin pursuing the only way he could become a "better lover": by focusing on his own sexual sensations.

Once again, we find that the route to intimacy is through accepting selfishness—your own and your partner's. In tandem masturbation, you never forget that first, *you are in control of your own sexuality* and second, *you and your partner are having separate sexual experiences together.* These are the two cardinal principles that allow you to move on to adventurous and intimate lovemaking.

By acknowledging that you alone are responsible for your sexual satisfaction, you can stop blaming your partner for an unsatisfactory sexual experience. But this also means that you are free from inhibiting criticism by your partner. You can stop being so focused on your partner's sexual responses that you never have any sexual pleasure of your own. Masturbation is the first step in accepting the fact that you own your sexuality. It's yours and the pleasures are yours. When you take the next step of sharing sex with your partner, you will be secure in that fact: you will know that you won't lose those pleasures when you share them.

One of the most liberating results of this exercise is that on a future night when one partner is overtired or sick, he can guilt-lessly say, "Hey, I'm exhausted, do you feel like doing it yourself while I watch?"

When your arrive at the point where you can be that free with one another, intimacy has replaced shame in your relationship.

"All this is fascinating in theory, Dagmar, but it's got nothing to do with reality. I mean, I've never even told my partner that I masturbate and for all I know she doesn't do it herself. I'm not sure I'm even ready to talk about it, let alone suddenly start doing it in front of each other."

I'm not surprised. In fact, I'm pretty sure that masturbation is a secret in most marriages, which is rather amazing when you think about it. I've seen hundreds of couples who have shared the same bed for umpteen years, raised children together, done their tax returns together, probed each other's souls together, but not once have they dared to bring up the "forbidden subject." When I start discussing masturbation with a couple in my office, frequently both partners will deny that they've ever done it since adolescence, yet when I see this pair separately, they will each "confess" that actually they masturbate regularly and always have. There are even some people who find it easier to admit an infidelity to each other than to admit that they masturbate.

The shame of masturbation runs deep in most of us. Rare indeed is the person who did not first masturbate under a cloud of disgrace. If his parents did not inform him that it was "self-abuse," surely some schoolyard friend told him that it would grow warts on his hands, stunt his growth, or make him grow up to be a pansy. And even those who grew beyond those awful myths as adults still clung to the more destructive myth that *masturbation is only for ugly and lonely people* and that successful people don't have to do "it" for themselves. "I don't need to do it," these men say. "I've got a wife for that."

In homes where sexual infrequency has become a problem,

admitting to your partner that you masturbate can be particularly humiliating.

"I guess I was sort of banking on her thinking that I'd lost all interest in sex," a husband in a relatively sexless marriage told me. "But then when we got to the tandem masturbation exercise I admitted that all along I've been doing it four and five times a week. I thought it was going to be a real slap in the face, but then she turned around and told me that she'd been doing the same thing and instead of feeling resentful, we both started laughing. I guess it was the relief of having the awful secret out in the open at last."

Indeed, most couples experience a rush of relief just by "confessing" their secret. Without fully realizing it, they have each been carrying a load of guilt around with them. The confession—often a *mutual* confession—begins to mitigate that guilt immediately. And the next step, of actually *demonstrating* your secret to one another, usually sets the rest of that guilt free.

"But maybe my partner really doesn't ever masturbate. Not everybody does, you know."

I know. But at the risk of being called perverse, I have to say that I think everybody should try masturbating once in a while. "Just to keep a hand in," as one of my witty colleagues says. Years ago, Masters and Johnson broke new ground by declaring that in order to start enjoying sex again we have to revive our early sexual experiences. They meant we should go back to petting, but in fact our earliest sexual experience was with ourselves and that is where we should begin. It can be a very healing experience, one that starts us feeling sexually alive again.

For people who have had no sex of any kind for a long time, I usually suggest starting immediately by masturbating alone once a day for a week. This is often all it takes to wake up the "numb middles" of people who have avoided sexual feelings for so long that turning themselves off has become a reflex. It's a start. It assures them that they do have a sex life, just not a mutual one yet. Changes in sexual responses begin alone. If you cannot become comfortable with these changes on your own, you will have trouble making these changes together with your partner. Or, as Woody Allen put it more positively, "I'm a terrific lover because I practice by myself a lot."

I recommend two very good books that detail how you can explore your own sexual feelings through solo masturbation: Lonnie Barbach's *For Yourself,* for women, and Bernie Zilbergeld's, *Male Sexuality,* for men.

"I still think it's going to be impossible to get myself to do this in front of my partner. Maybe my shame is irrational, but it's part of me."

It will be difficult, but not impossible. One way you can relieve much of your anxiety is by sticking to the rules: masturbate *simultaneously.* That way neither of you will feel so exposed; your partner is not focused on you.

Some of you may want to work up to the exercise gradually, say, first masturbating under the covers or turned away in the bed. Then next time you can reveal yourself a bit more, step by step until you are finally comfortably open with one another.

Look, I know you are going to resist doing this exercise every way you can. It is scary, no doubt about it. But it is an adventure that can be as exciting as the first time you made love. And it is a giant step toward intimacy.

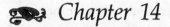 *Chapter 14*

Beautiful Fruit

Week Four

A young husband described to me what he called one of the great puzzles of life:

"I can still remember in detail the first time I touched a bare breast," he began. "It was a positively delirious moment. My girlfriend and I were kissing and I slipped my hand under her sweater, up her belly and then, oh God, what beautiful fruit! The smoothness of it! The softness of it! It was out of this world. I was fourteen years old and I was in heaven. I literally came right then and there.

"That was only fifteen years ago. Now I'm married to a woman with perfectly lovely breasts, but when I touch them I could be touching her elbow for all the excitement I feel. What happened to that beautiful fruit?"

I hear such laments frequently in my office. What happened to the thrill of that first kiss, that first touch of the breast, that first roll in the hay?

"Am I running out of endocrines?" one man asked me in all seriousness.

It is never possible to totally recapture the excitement of a first experience, whether it is the first bare breast touched or the first chocolate mousse eaten. Such experiences can only be perfectly unique and innocent once. But that does *not* mean that the only alternative is boredom and numbness. *That* is something we do to ourselves by blocking out our feelings. Our endocrines do not run out on us: we run out on our feelings. And part of what these exercises are all about is getting those feelings and a great deal of that thrill of "firstness" back again.

"Ah, now I understand why we weren't' allowed to touch breasts for three weeks. To make them forbidden fruit all over again! You've got us panting like fourteen-year-olds to break the taboo again. Pretty cheap trick."

Listen, if it works, it works. But it is not just the forbiddenness that has you panting to touch/be touched on the breasts. Chances are that over the years you have been so focused on stimulating breasts (and genitals) that you virtually excluded the rest of your body. Breasts were knobs that had to be turned to "tune in" a sexual response. They had to do all the work and so in time they lost sensitivity for both Toucher and Touchee. But after three weeks of the Sensual Exercises, your whole body is much more sensitive than it has been in years and your breasts are "rested," ready and yearning to join in.

This next week of the exercises, I want you to begin including breasts—but not genitals—in each of your three double sessions. Touchee, you decide exactly when you want your partner to touch your breasts. Put his hand there when you are ready. This means the Toucher cannot dive for the breasts first thing and totally focus on them to the exclusion of the rest of the body. That would just start bad habits all over again. No, get the rest of your body tingling first; that will make the touch of the breasts more ecstatic later.

Remember, the Touchee always remains in total control. If she (or he) is not happy with the *way* she is being touched, she is in charge of demonstrating exactly how she does want it done. She can do this by putting her hand over his and guiding him. Or she can show him what she wants by caressing her own breasts as an "object lesson." And when she wants to move from one mode of touching to another, she signals, too. But no lectures allowed, not a word. "Don't speak of love, *show me.*" Finally, if at any point she is uncomfortable or anxious, she retains the option to pick up the Toucher's hand and place it somewhere else altogether on her body.

The sad fact is that many women go through their entire marriages numbly allowing their husbands to touch their breasts in a way that they do not enjoy because they are too timid or frightened to ask for the kind of caresses they really want. Now is the chance to change all that. Some women find this stage of the exercises especially gratifying for precisely that reason.

"For the first time in eighteen years I could finally get Ralph to stop pinching my nipples and start teasing them lightly," Genevieve told me. "It's something I'd fantasized about for years, but if it hadn't been part of the exercise, I don't think I would have had the guts to ask him. And I don't think he would have taken it so well either."

Genevieve's husband could hardly be blamed for touching her breasts the "wrong way" if she kept the "right way" a secret from him. But with the help of the rules of the exercises, she broke the ice and showed him exactly what she wanted. For his part, Ralph had given up some control to be responsive to his wife's desires. In the end, both of them were happier. From then on in their relationship, "permission" was granted both of them to always show each other what they really wanted.

"I swear, I started loving Ralph more that very day," this woman told me. "Could that be possible?"

"Oscar Wilde once said that love is gratitude for pleasure," I replied. "In one day you went from enduring displeasure from your husband to getting pleasure from him. That certainly sounds like grounds for love to me."

The husband of another woman was totally amazed by his wife's response to their first breast-touching session.

"She pulled my head to her breasts and made it abundantly

clear that she wanted me to suck on her nipples," he told me. "I was flabbergasted. I mean, it's what I've been yearning to do for years, but I was positive she hated that. In fact, I distinctly remember her once stopping me from doing it."

"When was that?" I asked him.

The man rubbed his eyes for a moment, then smiled in embarrassment.

"About twenty years ago," he said.

This anecdote may sound comical, but I hear variations on it almost every week. One partner *once* told the other partner that she didn't like this or that and it's been a rule of their relationship chiseled in granite ever since. But the fact is our desires and responses change from day to day, not just from decade to decade. And probably no part of the female body is more subject to variability than the breasts; for most women, breast sensitivity changes constantly throughout the menstrual cycle. For example, many women experience breast soreness just before and during menstruation and do not want to have their breasts touched at all during that time. Furthermore, some women are simply more responsive in their breasts than other women; some can be brought to orgasm by breast stimulation while some rarely get turned on at all by it. I can say, however, that a great number of women who were originally in this "insensitive" group did find that their breasts become much more responsive during this stage of the exercises. It works the same as all the previous exercises work: the more control you feel you have, the more comfortable you get; and the more comfortable you feel, the more sensitive you get.

"But what if he caresses my breasts just the way I want and I don't get turned on?"

"And what if I caress her breasts just the way I want and I don't get an erection?"

Stop worrying about whether you are turned on or not. All you have to do is feel what you feel. Focus on these feelings.

Enjoy these feelings! You are still not going to go anywhere else with them, so that is all you can do.

And experiment as much as you can. See how many new sensations you can enjoy. You may just want your partner to touch your breasts with his hands, but maybe you want to see if you would enjoy his mouth and tongue, too. Perhaps you are curious about how his belly would feel against your breasts. His thighs, his buttocks. Maybe you would like him to eat whipped cream off of your breasts or to see what it feels like to have your nipples teased with a feather. Anything goes—if you want it to go. And now is the time to experiment with all the variations you have only fantasized about before.

One last point: I've been talking as if only women were sensitive in their breasts and nipples. Not so at all. One big surprise for many couples doing this exercise is the discovery that his nipples are every bit as sensitive and pleasurable as hers. Many men even find that their nipples become erect when they are sensually stimulated. Don't be embarrassed or succumb to the ridiculous thought that this is a feminine response. It is just one more sensual response available to you. It is just one more pleasure you can give each other.

Chapter 15

Show and Tell,
Touch and Go 🦀

Week Five

Doing sex is a perfect way to never see your own and your partner's genitals. You can get through the whole business complete with orgasm without ever having to look "down there." And if you are really skilled at doing sex, you never even have to touch "it" with your hands; you can get to your goal by remote control.

"Hold it right there, Dagmar, you're contradicting yourself again. I thought your major gripe with doing sex was that it was too focused on genitals."

That's right, doing sex is so focused on genital stimulation that it neglects all your other feelings. But at the same time, doing sex *distances* you from your own and your partner's genitals. You experience your genitals as being "down there" doing their thing, while your self remains "up here" in your head, waiting for the thrill to be relayed to it. You never really relate to your own or your partner's genitals as an integral part of yourselves. You never really love them.

"But I'm crazy about my genitals. They're the part of my body that give me the most pleasure. You're the one who has been ignoring them with your touch-everywhere-but-there exercises."

If you're so crazy about your genitals, why are you so reluctant to let your partner really see them? The sad truth is that deep inside, most of us feel if not ashamed at least insecure by the way our own genitals look. And a great many people are frightened by the way their partner's genitals look.

It all started with Adam and Eve and a few locally grown fig leaves. "Cover your nakedness!" their Maker admonished them and by nakedness He meant only one thing, genitalia. These were the body parts that should be hidden from the only other human being on Earth. We have been hearing the same admonition from our parents ever since. Call it modesty if you like, but modesty is precariously close to shame. As we grow older, the message gets clearer: wash your hands thoroughly after you touch yourself down there; never wear anybody else's underwear even if it's been laundered a thousand times. "Down there" is your body's toilet, its garbage department. Don't you understand? *It's dirty down there.*

Later on we get bombarded by another message of shame. The only genitals—especially female genitals—that we ever see on public displays are infinitely more beautiful than our own (or our partner's). How many times have you seen a painting of a nude with a large bush of pubic hair? No, the only pubic hair we ever really get an opportunity to study up close has been idealized to look like it belongs on an eleven-year-old girl. God help us, our own genitals do not look like that. Ours are hairy, fleshy, scraggly—anything but neat. We decide that we'd better keep this horrid thing out of sight—our own and our lover's. *Hey, it's ugly down there.*

On top of our own shame, we may have to deal with our partner's deep-seated fears about seeing and touching our genitals. There are many men who become overwhelmed with anxiety by the sight of a vagina: at some preconscious level they see it as a spider's web, a trap they'll never escape from, a chasm that can swallow them up. These men can only do sex if their partner's vagina is hidden from view. There are also many women who are frightened by the sight of a penis, especially an erect penis: it looks dangerous, scary, oversized—a weapon. Women with these fears would much rather deal with a penis under the covers and in the dark—or preferably not at all.

"Listen, if doing it under the covers is what it takes to have good sex, who cares? If it works, it works, as you always say."

But it doesn't work, not really. As long as we carry these shames and fears with us, we can never really make love. *As long as we don't really accept our most intimate parts, we can never be completely intimate with each other.*

So before we start to include touching genitals in the Sensual Exercises, we have to get to know our genitals—intimately.

Sometime before your next double session, I want each of you to stand alone and naked in front of a full-length mirror and give yourself a complete once-over. (If you don't own a full-length mirror, go out and buy one; it's time you saw your body as a whole instead of as the sum of isolated parts.) As your look yourself over from head to toe, focus on what you like about your body. You *know* what you don't like; you've focused on *that* a hundred times. This time, "accentuate the positive and eliminate the negative," as the old song goes. What's your best "angle"? Say what you like about it out loud. What do you like about your eyes? Your mouth? What do you like about your chest or breasts? For once, don't dwell on your perception that your breasts are too small or too large, too wide or too low. Cup your hands underneath them and announce to the world what is particularly attractive about them. Don't automatically compare them to the breasts on the cover of the current issue of *Cosmopolitan.* In fact, don't compare them to anybody else's. Even if you've burdened yourself with a miserable self-image all these years, I know there is something you really do like about your breasts, something you may have been too embarrassed to admit to yourself ever before—say, the sensuous shadow of your cleavage or the smooth texture of the skin around your nipples. For once, flaunt what is beautiful about your body instead of always reflexively hiding what you do not find beautiful about it. Overcome your hammered-in fear of being "too proud." Banish all embarrassment. Find at least *five* things about your body that you can brag about and sing out your praises loud and clear. Finish the exercise by telling your reflection, "I love you."

"This is all too Pollyanna-ish for me, Dagmar. I can't delude myself into thinking I'm looking good just by practicing some phony positive thinking. I'm still a realist and proud of it."

Why is it that realists only think negative perceptions are real? I'm not asking you to deny what you find unattractive about your body; I'm only asking you for once to focus on what is attractive. That's real, too. Look, many people have trouble taking pride in their bodies, but what exactly do you have to lose?

Now we come to the hard part: taking a good gander at your genitals. The very prospect can make the most sober of us dizzily uncomfortable. To get a complete perspective it helps to have a hand mirror. Men, check it all out: take a look at your perineum —that sensitive ridge of skin between your anus and your scrotum; cup your testicles and feel their weight; feel how they change with the temperature of the room; roll back your foreskin and look the tip of your penis straight in the eye. Describe everything you see out loud, like a doctor dictating a physical examination. Women, you have more nooks and crannies to explore. It might help to put the hand mirror on the floor and squat over it. Spread your labia majora—the outer lips of your vagina —and peer inside. Pull the hood back from your clitoris and examine it as closely as possible. It is truly remarkable how many women go through life without once seeing this, their most sensitive spot. Say hello to it. Become comfortable with it.

Happily, just the mere act of objectively examining our genitals can make us much more comfortable with them. In reality, they are neither as dirty nor as ugly as we imagined them.

"I was literally terrified of looking at my genitals," one woman told me after she tried this exercise. "I had been hearing it called a 'box' and a 'beard' for so long, I expected it to look like something out of the *The Little Shop of Horrors.* But now I've decided it's kind of sweet-looking, all pink and everything."

Another woman told me that she had always been embarrassed because her vagina didn't look like the "innocent flower bud" usually depicted on statues. Then she took a good long look at hers during this exercise.

"One thing I discovered is that I'm not made of marble after all," she laughed. "Maybe mine's not as perfect-looking as Venus de Milo's, but it's got the advantage of being soft and warm and rosy."

Now it's time for Show and Tell. Just before you get started with your next Sensual Exercise double session, I want you to share the Mirror Exercise with one another. Standing naked next to each other in front of the full-length mirror, take turns describing yourself to your partner. Once again, accentuate the positive. If you are absolutely too embarrassed to only "brag" about your good points, throw in a few bad points, too—but don't get carried away with that side of the balance. While your partner is talking about his own body, *don't say a word.* No corrections, not even compliments. You know what you like about your partner's body, now hear what he has to say about it.

When your partner comes to his genitals, you will both probably want to move the "examination" to the bed. Get down between your partner's legs and take a real close look. Put on your reading glasses and use a penlight or flashlight to peer inside. Let your partner guide your hand as you "poke around" exploring his "private parts." Neither of you should be focusing on feelings of arousal at this point—that's not the idea just yet—so for heaven's sake, don't get uptight if you are *not* aroused. You are just making friends with your partner's genitals. Get used to handling it. You'll both be nervous and skittish at first, I can assure you, but you can have fun with this part of the exercise if you try. Take the pressure off by making it into a game. Play doctor, explorer, or, as one inventive husband did, play ventriloquist.

"When he got to his penis," his wife told me, "he started waving it around with his hand and talking in this funny voice, 'Hello, I'm Dick, Jonathon's pecker. Don't I know you from somewhere?' He absolutely cracked me up."

Getting to know each other's genitals is one of the simplest but often most profound acts of intimacy I know.

"I haven't felt that shy with anyone since I was a teenager," one woman reported. "It was like I was naked for the first time in front of Clayton and that kind of felt—innocent in a way, like we were really sharing something new with each other."

For this woman and her husband, Show and Tell was the prelude to a new intimacy in their relationship. They had nothing more to hide.

"That's just wonderful, Dagmar, but this all sounds about as sexy as making a snowman. It's starting to feel like we're in a hospital laboratory, not in a conjugal bedroom. You're determined to take all the mystery and romance out of sex, aren't you."

I'm not taking the mystery and romance out of sex, just the shame and fear. My goal is to desensitize you to any aversions, hidden or otherwise, you may have to your own and your partner's genitals. By having a good look at these "private parts" without the pressures of sexual performance hanging over you, you can calmly make your peace with them. No, they aren't dirty or devouring, not ugly or dangerous. They are marvelous parts of our bodies which we can share with one another. Nothing sexy has been lost, but something loving has been gained.

Now that you are both in bed, you are ready to start your first Sensual Exercise for the week. Like last week, take an absolute minimum of fifteen minutes touching/being touched everywhere *except* breasts and genitals. Making love is a *total body* experience, not just a "hot spots" experience. Next, spend some time caressing your partner's breasts. Take your time. Don't look at the clock. Be as creative as you *both* desire—use your lips, your tongue, a feather, whipped cream. As always, focus on your *own* feelings, not on your partner's responses.

When your partner is ready, he will reach for your hand and bring it to his genitals. Remember, the Touchee is in total control of *where, how,* and *how long* he wants his genitals touched. The first three genital-touching sessions, *the Touchee must keep his hand over the Toucher's hand all the time it is in the genital area.* I do not mean just for corrections; I mean all the time. The Touchee is in full charge. The Touchee is teacher.

Touchee, for now, think of the whole experience as *stimulating yourself using your partner's hand.* You know what you feel; you know what you want. Now give it to yourself. Don't be shy or embarrassed or ashamed—you are going to return the favor to your partner in just a little while. And listen, you are about to teach your partner something that he has been dying to know: *how to give you what you want when you want it.*

It is truly sad how a person can spend years in a relationship afraid to show his partner exactly what would give him pleasure. He would rather endure decades of unfulfilled fantasies than simply take his partner's hand and demonstrate that this—say, lightly bouncing his testicles on her fingertips or tickling the underside of the head of his penis—is what he longs for right now. Coming out and directly asking for it feels too selfish and self-indulgent or worse, too blatantly sensual. But the awful paradox is, his partner probably feels like a failure because she wants to give him pleasure but she doesn't know how.

But how in heaven's name are we supposed to know exactly what will give our partner pleasure if he does not tell us—or more to the point, *show* us? Are we supposed to know by intuition?

"I thought that's what love is supposed to be all about," a young woman once said to me. "If he really loved me, he'd know just where to touch me and when. He'd know exactly how to turn me on."

"Should he know exactly when you are going to sneeze, too?" I asked her. "And the moment you're hungry and precisely what you want to eat? Give him a break. He's not inside your skin. Show him what you want. Only then can he show you that he loves you by giving you exactly what you want."

Let's resolve to put an end to this ridiculous secret between you. From now on: show what you want; get what you want; give your partner what she wants. And remember, what we want is constantly changing. You cannot memorize your partner's desires, but you can always communicate to your partner what you desire now. It's really that simple. And it's going to make you love each other much more than you ever have before.

"Just a second, Dagmar, it's not that simple at all. What if I take my wife's hand and put it, say, on my testicles and she freaks out? Do you think that's going to make us love each other madly, too?"

That's a risk, I grant you. But it's a risk you should both be willing to take right now. Otherwise, neither of you may ever get or give the pleasure you deserve; neither of you may ever grow. I don't believe that you should compel your partner to do anything she does not want to do, that you should force her hand against her will. But by the same token, now is a chance for you, the Toucher, to overcome some important inhibitions. Try regarding your hand as totally passive as your partner guides it to where he wants it. For a little while, allow yourself to dissociate from your hand, numb yourself to its sensations. Then, as your initial anxiety and skittishness subside, gradually let the feeling come back and focus on what it feels like to touch him in the "forbidden" spot. Not so bad, is it? Just another part of the body. You really can desensitize yourself to an inhibition that easily, that quickly. Who knows? You may even start enjoying it yourself, right then and there. If not this time, maybe next time.

There is another danger couples sometimes run up against at this point: one partner learns that he has been touching his partner "wrong" all these years and he gets sullen and defensive.

"He's always gone right for my clitoris, wiggled it around harder and faster than I really want, trying to get me to orgasm as quickly as possible," a middle-aged wife told me. "Here was my chance to show him how I like it—kind of slow, light circles around my clitoris until it pulls back under the hood and it's not so sensitive and that's when I want the hard and fast stuff. So I guided his hand that way. Well, all of a sudden he gets this glum look on his face like I've hurt this little boy's feelings. What a turn-off. I called an end to the session right then and there."

"Don't worry about him," I told her. "His reaction is a hard one to ignore, but you should try. In the process, he just might grow up a little bit and discover that there's no possible way he could have known what you wanted until now."

FIRST GENITAL SESSION

This first session, include genitals as if they were just another part of the body, no more erogenous than, say, an elbow. We are not aiming for arousal this time. This is just going to be an extension of Show and Tell. Touchee, if you feel at all anxious, don't be afraid to move your partner's hand to another part of your body for a while; then bring it back to your genitals when you are feeling more relaxed. The idea is to feel perfectly comfortable.

"All this and no orgasms? How much more of this torture am I supposed to endure?"

Just forgo orgasm this one last time. (If you find it that tortuous, you can always finish off your double session with tandem masturbation.) But for now I want you to fully experience what it's like to linger with arousal. Focus on those feelings of excitement and pleasure building up inside you. Feel them radiating all over your body—in your belly and thighs, your breasts, your anus, the back of your neck, the tips of your toes. These are the very sensations that most of us have habitually short-circuited by always shooting straight for orgasm. This time there is not going to be an orgasm, so you might as well slow down and drink in all the pleasure your partner is giving you. For many people, doing this exercise finally makes the whole purpose of this program click into place. They learn the ultimate lesson about sensual pleasure: it is not a means to an end, it is an end in itself.

"I don't think I've ever been so turned on in my life," one husband reported after his first genital-touching session. "I was tuning in to sensations I'd never felt before. Tingly stuff all over the old bod. Sure, part of me was dying to come, but I didn't want all these feelings to come to an end either."

"Next time you can have your cake and eat it, too," I told him. "But you'll know you don't gain anything by hurrying your orgasm."

Lingering with arousal provides one of the essential differences between doing sex and making love. In a prolonged state of arousal, sexual sensations and emotional feelings flow together.

"Before you get carried away, Dagmar, let me ask you one question: What happens if she caresses my genitals and I don't get turned on? What if I don't get an erection? What if there's no arousal to linger with?"

Don't worry about it. Just enjoy the pleasure you do feel. And if you are still anxious, simply move your partner's hand to another part of your body. This is not a challenge, not a contest.

Some of you may take several sessions before you are relaxed and comfortable enough to become aroused in this exercise. There is no time limit on when you should get turned on.

SECOND GENITAL SESSION

If you both experienced arousal during the first genital session, now is the time for you to experiment with that arousal—feel it build and subside and build again. No, this is not some perverse game I'm prescribing; it's a way to double and triple and quadruple your pleasure. But before I explain how to "play" with arousal, let me assure you that, yes, this time orgasms are part of the program. Yet try to put it off as long as you can. If you must have a goal, it should be this: see how long you can linger with arousal before you have an orgasm.

As in your first genital session, Touchee, have your partner spend a good long time caressing the rest of your body before you let him move to your breasts and genitals. As before, you are in total control of where and how your partner touches you; keep your hand over his continuously in the genital area. But this time, after you have lingered with arousal for a while, move your partner's hand to another part of your body letting your arousal subside. Men, that means allowing your erection to fade away before you bring your partner's hand back to your penis.

"And start all over again? What is this, Dagmar, some new kind of torture you've devised?"

Not new torture—new security! Because, lo and behold, your arousal—and your erection—will come back again. And again and again. Each man needs to be reassured of that fact every once in a while whether or not he has ever had a night when he "failed to perform." Almost every man harbors a secret fear of losing his erection and losing it *for good.* The anxiety born of that fear is one of the main reasons why men tend to rush through sex—they want to get to orgasm before they risk losing their erections. Once again, feelings get sacrificed to sexual anxiety.

This exercise desensitized that anxiety in the simplest way I can think of: you prove to yourself that your erection is ready and willing to come back when you want it.

Many women harbor a similar fear. They are convinced that when they lose arousal, it's gone for the night. Goodbye and good luck until next time. And if they think that the reason they've lost their last chance for some satisfying sex that night is because their lover took a rest break or changed hands, they end up feeling pretty unloving toward him. What a waste. A woman's arousal doesn't have to disappear for good any more than a man's does. You don't lose "it." Yes, it dims; your clitoris may become less engorged and sensitive for a while. But the arousal is still there waiting to be "revved up" when you bring your partner's hand back for more stimulation. And what's more, this time around you will probably arrive at a higher plateau of arousal. Again, move your partner's hand away for a while and then bring it back. The arousal is still there waiting to shoot up another level. When you are finally secure that your arousal does not disappear during these "breaks," you will find it much easier to linger with arousal and not to hurry on to orgasm.

"All my life I've thought of orgasm as a brass ring on the merry-go-round," one woman reported to me after experiencing this exercise. "If I didn't grab it first time around, I might never have another chance. So whenever I started feeling turned on, I'd try to have an orgasm as quickly as possible. Now I know what I was missing all those years. For one thing, I was missing really powerful orgasms—the kind you build up to for hours."

Allowing arousal to come and go is also a boon for those women who have always worried that they take too long to reach orgasm. Many of these women were in the habit of just giving up when they were not able to climax within some self-imposed time limit. Now, after learning to "enjoy the trip," they were having orgasms almost every time.

When you finally come to the point where you can't resist any longer and want to have an orgasm now, be sure to keep your hand on top of your partner's all the way to the end *and after.* Most of us find it uncomfortable or even painful to be stimulated on the clitoris or the glans of the penis immediately after orgasm, yet many people resist taking their partner's hand away at this point because they are afraid they'll "break the mood" or hurt their partner's feelings. Nonsense. You are still in charge and your partner still wants to know what will give you the most pleasure. You may just want to be hugged now. Or perhaps touched lightly on the back or buttocks or legs. The session need not come to an end just because you have had an orgasm. Keep drinking in pleasure. Let your feelings flow.

I believe it is important for all women to know many routes to orgasm, not just intercourse. It gives you and your partner options and those options can take a load of anxiety off both of you. Orgasm via manual stimulation by your partner should be one of those options. It's always there whether he is up for sex at the same time you are or not. As one of my colleagues says, "The best thing about manual sex is that it's always handy."

If you have trouble having an orgasm with his hand, first try using your own hand while he rests his on top of yours. It may take a few tries before you are comfortable enough to let go and have an orgasm. Next, go on to putting his hand on the hood of your clitoris. Hold his hand and move your body against it. That way you are still in control. Next session you will be able to let him take over stimulation. Again, you may need a few of these sessions before you are comfortable enough to reach orgasm.

Speaking of comfort: men, when you are fondling your partner's clitoris, rest on your wrist and let your fingers do the stroking. There is no sense getting worn out just when the fun is beginning.

Here I go being a sex therapist and teaching technique after swearing that most technique is for sexual mechanics, not lovers. But believe me, these techniques are the kind that relieve sexual anxiety and let your other feelings come through—especially loving feelings.

"When I learned to have an orgasm with his hand, I finally stopped feeling so dependent on his mood," one wife told me. "I didn't always have to wait until he was turned on when I was feeling sexy. I could ask for an orgasm whenever I wanted one. Just knowing that makes me one happy—and loving—woman."

THIRD GENITAL SESSION

If you were both comfortable with your last session, see how you can stretch your boundaries even farther this time. Perhaps you'll want to change your location again, say to the living room where the Toucher can kneel on the rug in front of the sofa where the Touchee lies languorously with her legs spread wide. Be inventive. Use props—a feather boa, a fur coat, scented oils. As a prelude to oral-genital contact, you may want to "garnish" your partner's genitals with something yummy like raspberry jam or marshmallow fluff. Go for it.

Many people become anxious by the very prospect of oral-genital sex because they are worried that their partner's genitals are not clean. I have a subtle method for overcoming this anxiety: wash them yourself! That's right, take your partner to the shower, lather him up—especially his penis, and make sure he is squeaky clean. But I warn you, some of you may end up having such a good time that you stay in there until the hot water runs out.

I know one woman in her sixties who had fantasized about oral-genital sex all her adult life, but she had never dared ask her husband to do it to her because she could not bring herself to do it to him—all because she felt genitals were unclean and "unfit for consumption." I urged her and her husband into the shower with a bar of soap. It was all it took to reduce her anxiety enough to get on with fulfilling her fantasy.

"Now we've got a new problem," her husband said to me, winking. "She never lets me take a shower alone."

In this third session, as always build to breast and genital contact slowly and gradually. There's no hurry now. You know there's pleasure waiting for you *every step of the way.* Touchee, stay in charge, hands on your partner's hands, especially in the genital area. Play with arousal. Let it build. It you want your partner to caress your genitals with his lips and mouth, gently pull him to you. Keep your hands on his head and guide him, maneuvering him to just the spot where you want him, signaling him with your movements to go slower or faster, lifting him away the moment you feel uncomfortable. You may be breaking through boundaries here, but you are always in control.

Now is a perfect opportunity for a woman who has never had two orgasms in a row to go for it. The key, as always, is staying in control of the experience. Guide your partner well. Steer him away from your clitoris immediately after your first orgasm and only bring him back to it after you've felt your clitoris pull back under its hood again. Linger with arousal as long as you can this time, but then let this second orgasm happen. Some women harbor the illusion that only specially gifted women are capable of multiple orgasms. Not so. The only "gift" you need is the belief that you deserve pleasure and the willingness to take it. That's a gift you can give yourself—with a little help from your friend.

Many couples will find the move to these genital sessions difficult. Suddenly, these "love sessions" have become "real sex" again and all your old anxieties about sex may return with a vengeance. You may find yourself bringing out all your old avoidance techniques to deal with these anxieties: starting a fight just before the session begins or worse, "forgetting" to initiate altogether. What this resistance means is that you are getting very close to changing. Don't give up now. These exercises are flushing out fears and anxieties you may have never been aware of before. Pushing beyond them is the only way that you—and your relationship—will grow.

WEEK SIX

By now, most of you will know from experience what it means to say that the key to intimacy is selfishness and the key to free-flowing feelings is control. These are not paradoxes after all: they are the secrets to giving and taking pleasure; they are the secrets of making love.

For the past five weeks, you have taken turns being Toucher and Touchee, giver and taker. You have discovered that you do not "fall apart" or "get swallowed up" or "die of shame" when you allow yourself unlimited "pointless pleasure." On the contrary, most people feel more integrated and alive and loving. By taking your turn at being "passive," you have learned how to focus on your own feelings and sensations rather than always watching your partner's responses. You have taken that most liberating of risks: allowing your partner to be separate from you. Now the trick is to hold on to that "selfish" focus as you return to simultaneous lovemaking.

But first a word about simultaneity. Somewhere along the line romantic love became saddled with the absurd notion that lovers should always do everything and feel everything at exactly the same time. If she's stroking my face, I should be stroking her now, too. If she's feeling aroused, I certainly should be aroused, too. And, of course, if she's having an orgasm, I should be having one too, *at precisely the same moment.* The only good orgasms are simultaneous orgasms. Otherwise, our love is imperfect. Otherwise, we must be doing something wrong.

Humbug!

For me, real intimacy always allows us to move from passive Taker to active Giver and back again. The fact is you can never focus so completely on your own pleasurable sensations as when you are just passively drinking them in. But, of course, there is a special joy in mutuality, too. It is like a dance: you respond to each other; his touch makes me want to touch him, back and forth, round and round. This is altogether different from a compulsive response. You are resounding to your own feelings, not to some sense of obligation. You are still focused on what you feel yourself, not on what you think your partner is feeling.

When you do your Sensual Exercises this coming week, start playing with this mutuality. You will still take turns being Touchee and Toucher, and the Touchee will still remain in control, but this time when the spirit moves him, he can respond. He can touch back. Yet the moment he finds himself losing touch with his own sensations, he should return to being totally passive again until he recovers that focus. Again, move as gradually as you can to caressing breasts and genitals. Linger with each sensation as long as possible. When you come to genitals, many of you will want to alternate being Giver and Taker again rather than dilute your focus by aiming for simultaneous orgasms. All that means is that you are enjoying each other more than ever. You are loving the pleasure you are giving each other. And you feel free enough to take in as much of that pleasure as you can.

"I felt like that girl in *Dirty Dancing*," one woman reported to me at this stage of the exercise. "All these years I'd been doing the 'right moves' in bed, but it's like somebody else was doing the choreography. I had to listen to my heartbeat, feel my own feelings, and then all of a sudden I was just inside my body, 'dancing' without thinking about it. I guess that's what making love is really all about, isn't it?"

Indeed it is.

WEEK SEVEN

In the East, there are yogis who recommend that neither partner move at all during the *first hour* of sexual intercourse. How's that for lingering with arousal! Well, before anyone gets overwhelmed with competitive performance anxiety by this piece of information, remember that these are the same yogis who can snooze on a bed of nails; they've made a career of mastering their bodies. Still, just the knowledge that a human being is capable of lovemaking that is this slowed down is a healthy reminder to all of us. In the West, too many of us have been going to the opposite extreme of one-minute sex: the instant intercourse begins, we thrust away fast and furious, aiming for orgasm. And we end up missing most of the pleasures we could have had along the way—sensual and emotional as well as sexual.

Let's change all that now.

But before I offer a few yogic hints of my own about intercourse, I want to clear up a bit of linguistic confusion that has been plaguing us all for years: the absurd notion that sexual intercourse is the only activity that qualifies as "making love." To my mind, everything you've been doing these past six weeks is making love—including those sensual sessions without orgasms. Intercourse is just another option, another way of giving and receiving pleasure, another way of achieving intimacy. Intercourse is not the primary goal of this program, not your crowning achievement or final reward. Feelings, however you get them going again, are your reward. *That* is the love you make.

In this week's first sensual session, once again go through all the stages slowly before you get to touching genitals. Don't skip anything, not a part of your body, not a single sensation. It has been over a month since you've had intercourse, so we are going to approach it slowly and from a new "angle." It is time for what I call "a nice visit."

When you both have been playing with arousal for a good long time, let your partner (male) lie flat on his back while you (female) straddle him on your knees. Now take his penis at a forty-five-degree angle toward his upper body and gently insert *just the tip* into your vagina. Make like yogis—neither of you move. Focus on every sensation you feel. Stay with this for a while and then take his penis out again. That's it; the first "visit" is over. Return to stroking one another. You may want to come back for another visit later on, but resist full insertion of the penis today. Linger with arousal for as long as you can before you move to orgasms; obviously, no orgasms through intercourse this time.

The "nice visit" sounds simple and perhaps a little silly, but many women and men have told me that it was about as close as they have come to feeling the sensations of their "first time" all over again. They were able to focus on the wonder of their genitals touching without immediately switching that focus to the orgasm this touching was supposed to produce.

"I'd forgotten that marvelous shock of just feeling a penis inside me," one middle-aged woman told me with a little laugh. "By golly, I felt like a forty-six-year-old virgin."

This woman was tuning in to sensations that she had abandoned years ago to numbing sexual routines.

"Listen, I'm not a yogi—so what happens if I lose my erection during this no-moving-allowed visit of yours?"

What happens is that you allow yourself to keep enjoying everything you are feeling—both of you. Your penis does not go numb the moment your erection softens, nor does the tip stop feeling pleasant to her inside the opening of her vagina. By now I trust you've discovered that lovemaking does not have to come to an abrupt and miserable halt the moment an erection shows signs of softening. That erection will be back—probably the moment you stop worrying about it and start focusing again on what you feel.

But my guess is that you may be surprised to discover that you don't have to keep your penis stimulated every second for it to remain erect. The sensations are still there—that's what the yogis teach us. You just have to relax and focus on them.

🙐

Next session, repeat the nice visit, but very gradually pull your partner's penis completely inside you. Again, no movement. Focus on every sensation. Feel his pulse inside you. Feel his testicles against you . . . Feel the way you fill her. Feel her warmth and smooth wetness . . . Both of you *take a good look at the way you are joined together.* For some of you, this may be the first time you have actually seen your genitals conjoined. Over the years you may have been doing sex under wraps, in the dark, or with your eyes closed, inhibited about visually acknowledging what is going on "down there." Now you are ready to allow yourself to marvel at this sight. It can make your sexuality real in a way you may never have experienced it before. Veils of residual denial fall away. *This is happening now.* It can be an incredibly erotic moment. And it can be a moment of intense intimacy.

"It was the first time I felt his penis was truly there for me," one young wife told me. "I felt like a lovely hostess who had invited him inside and I could ask him to leave whenever I wanted to. This was for me, too—not just something that was being done to me."

This woman had just realized that when it came to intercourse, she had always relinquished ownership of her vagina to her husband. Like so many women, she had assumed that intercourse was basically for her man and her anger at feeling invaded and controlled by him had blocked out her loving feelings for him. This simple, nice visit turned out to be the most loving interaction they had had in years. Suddenly, her vagina belonged to her again—it was for her pleasure, too. Finally, she was able to use it to make love.

Now it's time to "go all the way." You can start moving and let go to orgasm. Now you don't have to hold back anymore. Again, I ask the woman to be on top and take care of inserting the penis. In most cases, the man has had most of the responsibility for intercourse; now it is the woman's turn to feel in control. More women have orgasms in the on-top position because they feel freer. Men, here's a chance to wallow in some passivity. Enjoy the view and let her do the work.

One woman who had never been on top before described her first experience to me: "When I finally got up my nerve and climbed on top of him this tremendous feeling of power came over me and I really started to get turned on. I looked down and Bob was smiling, cheering me on. I came with him inside me for the first time since we got married a million years ago. And God, I felt like I had fallen in love with him all over again."

In your next session, approach insertion from the side position for maximum freedom of movement for both of you. (In this position, one of the woman's legs is on top of her partner and one beneath him. Pull the leg that is underneath up into his hip cavity so that your bones don't jut against each other.) Don't move for a moment, but then begin slowly, always focusing on your sensations and feelings, not on some preconceived idea of how you should be moving or how your partner wants you to move. Listen to your heartbeat. You are on your own—together.

This is where I stop giving specific instructions and recipes. As I said at the beginning of this book, I don't believe in sexual technique per se. I don't recommend special "erotic" positions or diagram erogenous zones. I don't even suggest swinging from the chandeliers—I leave that to my more athletic-minded colleagues. I don't think there are any "secret pleasures" that you cannot discover for yourself. You are your own "expert." Now that you can freely and unashamedly tune into you own sensations, you know exactly what pleasures you want and where and when and how you want them. And happily, these pleasures will never be a secret again—especially not from your loving partner.

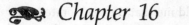 *Chapter 16*

The Love You Make

"I want to celebrate!" people often tell me when they come to the end of my program. "I want to have a graduation party! Better yet, a second wedding ceremony! I feel like we're starting our relationship all over again."

These are the happiest moments in my job. I still get all teary when I see that the process has worked once again and two people have learned to enjoy each other to the fullest. For a little while I indulge myself in the fantasy that Cupid, after all, is a sex therapist.

Indeed, this is the time for a couple to celebrate their relationship. A little vacation seems in order, if only an overnighter at a local motel. But a more enduring celebration that many couples choose now is to make their home a more loving and sensual place.

"I wanted to buy something festive for us," one woman told me on the phone. "So I went out and bought some black silk sheets for our bed. And then I found myself drifting over to the lingerie department where I got a black silk nightie to match."

This woman's husband surprised her that same evening with a gift of his own—a record of *Bolero*.

"He says it's his new theme song," his wife told me, laughing. "He says it starts slow and lingers with arousal longer than any piece he knows."

Many women and men have told me that they celebrated their new sensuality by buying new clothes that feel soft and sensual against their skin or by buying bath oils and bubble beads for long, leisurely baths.

"I never had a problem spending money on myself," one woman told me. "I could buy dress-for-success suits at three bills a shot, but God forbid I should buy a pair of silk panties just because they felt voluptuous. Well, yesterday I went out and bought an even dozen pair of silk panties—each in a different color."

One husband decided that what he and his wife needed for the "complete sensual bedroom" was a little refrigerator, "one you can raid when you're stark naked without having to worry about the kids seeing you."

"It's really for his supply of whipped cream," this man's wife told me, grinning. "Starting about the second week of the exercises, it became an indispensable part of our lovemaking."

Another husband went straight to the hardware store to "redecorate" his home for his newfound love life.

"I bought locks for every door in the house, including the kitchen and dining room," he told me. "That may not sound romantic to some people, but Jennifer was more thrilled than if I'd brought home a dozen roses. At last we could make love in any room in the house without having to worry about a junior intruder crashing in on us."

In the same spirit, another husband celebrated their "graduation" by buying venetian blinds for the living-room windows of their apartment.

"I was reclaiming the living-room sofa for our sex life," he said, winking. "Although I do hate to disappoint the neighbors."

Other couples have told me that although they feel like celebrating the new intimacy they've started experiencing, they are frightened it won't last.

"Nothing this good has ever lasted before," a young wife who had experienced orgasms with her husband for the first time told me. "I'm terrified that in a few months we'll be Ma and Pa Numbness again."

"You can make your new lovemaking last the rest of your life," I told her. "All you have to remember is that you can always go back to the beginning with exercise one and your feelings will be there waiting for you."

In fact, many couples do find some old problem or symptom suddenly reappearing just as they reach the end of my program. I call it the let's-see-if-the-old-defenses-still-work encore: a former premature ejaculator suddenly comes in a minute all over again; a former preorgasmic woman suddenly "can't feel anything" all over again. It's a way of testing ourselves—and torturing ourselves. But, thank goodness, after completing the program we all know that we are in control—all we have to do is take the necessary steps to get back to our feelings. You know that you are really cured of a bad habit or symptom when you are secure that you can go back and fix it yourself.

All of us will find ourselves coming back to elements of these exercises again and again. Many "graduates" of my program still regularly take turns being Initiator so that they will not get stuck in old habits. And many still like to enjoy regular sessions of body stroking without moving to genitals or orgasms.

"I know the sex will never go away now," a wife told me. "But I need to feel the same way about the tender, comforting stuff, too. And now that that doesn't frighten either of us anymore, it's become the touchstone of our relationship."

"Hands-on" demonstrations of exactly where and how a lover wants to be touched usually becomes incorporated into the ongoing lovemaking of a graduate couple, too. It becomes a natural and un-self-conscious part of their loving agreement to give each other all the pleasure they can.

Some couples make tandem masturbation a regular part of their love life; "Just to shock ourselves back to reality when we need it," as one man put it. And some couples tell me that whenever they have intercourse they now like to start with a little "nice visit." "It's become our way of saying to each other, 'Hello, I'm right here, off on this adventure with you.'"

But above all, the element of these exercises that I am happy to say stays with all of my graduates is the joyful confidence to be able to open the door, walk up or roll over and say, *"Now. I want to be touched now, darling."*

That will always be the beginning of the best lovemaking there is.

ABOUT THE AUTHOR

Swedish-born Dagmar O'Connor studied with Masters and Johnson in St. Louis. She is a practicing sex therapist in New York City where she is Director of the Sexual Therapy Program in the Department of Psychiatry at St. Luke's-Roosevelt Hospital Center, and she is a lecturer in psychiatry at Columbia University. She has practiced sex therapy for more than fifteen years.